GENERAL EDUCATION AND STUDENT TRANSFER

Fostering Intentionality and Coherence in State Systems

Edited by Robert Shoenberg

A Publication of the Greater Expectations Initiative

Vincennes University
Shake Learning Resources Center
Vincennes, In 47591-9986

 *Association
of American
Colleges and
Universities*

1818 R Street, NW, Washington, DC 20009-1604

Copyright © 2005 by the Association of American Colleges and Universities.
All rights reserved.

ISBN: 0–9763576–3–1

To order additional copies of this publication or to find out about other AAC&U publications,
visit www.aacu.org, e-mail pub_desk@aacu.org, or call 202.387.3760.

Cover photo: Elizabethtown College

The contents of this book were developed under a grant from the Fund for the Improvement of
Postsecondary Education, (FIPSE), U.S. Department of Education. However, those contents
do not necessarily represent the Department of Education, and you should not assume
endorsement by the Federal Government.

Contents

Preface...v

Acknowledgments..vii

1. Greater Expectations for Student Transfer
   Seeking Intentionality and the Coherent Curriculum
   By Robert Shoenberg 1

2. Faculty Collaboration and Statewide General Education Reform
   The Case of Utah
   By Ann Leffler, Philip I. Kramer, Norman L. Jones, and Phyllis Safman 25

3. Providing System Leadership for Student Success
   The Case of Georgia
   By Dorothy Zinsmeister 35

4. Building Statewide Partnerships for Student Success
   The Case of Maryland
   By Nancy S. Shapiro, Teri Hollander, and Jennifer Vest Frank.....................45

5. Intentionality and Coherence in Undergraduate General Education
   What Have We Learned?
   By Martin Finkelstein..55

About the Authors...69

Preface

Fostering a coherent set of general intellectual skills and developing capacities for knowledgeable citizenship are widely recognized overarching goals of baccalaureate education in the twenty-first century. With these goals in mind, in 2002 the Association of American Colleges and Universities (AAC&U) issued *Greater Expectations: A New Vision for Learning as a Nation Goes to College*, a report calling for the creation of a New Academy focused on providing students with an engaged, empowering, and practical liberal education.

The *Greater Expectations* report recommends that "colleges and universities place new emphasis on educating students to become intentional learners" by helping them develop "self-awareness about the reason for study, the learning process itself, and how education is used" (21). It further recognizes that to educate intentional learners, institutions of higher education need to become far more purposeful in their educational practices and programs. But nearly 60 percent of college graduates now attend multiple institutions before earning a degree. Creating a clear sense of purpose and a coherent program as students move among institutions has become an important new challenge for American higher education.

This publication reports on Greater Expectations for Student Transfer, a project supported by a grant from the Fund for the Improvement of Postsecondary Education (FIPSE) that allowed AAC&U and three statewide organizations to explore the problem of student transfer in the context of the Greater Expectations initiative. We chose to attack the problem at the state level because it seemed to us that, with so many students attending multiple institutions within the same state, state higher education systems and governing or coordinating boards were the only possible guarantors of programmatic coherence. The three states involved in the project—Georgia, Maryland, and Utah—along with a few others, have made a good start on defining clearly the purposes of their statewide requirements and conveying those intentions to faculty members, students, and advisers. This publication surveys the status of state-level efforts across the country and chronicles the successes and frustrations of the three states that participated in the project.

—Robert Shoenberg

Acknowledgments

Any effort, any innovation—particularly one played out on as large a field as this one—requires the work and good will of many people. Literally hundreds of administrators and faculty members played a role in Greater Expectations for Student Transfer, giving their time and attention to the project even though the outcomes of their work were uncertain. AAC&U thanks them for their work in helping to create a more purposeful education for all students, transfer and otherwise.

The people who worked most closely and extensively with the project are also the authors of the chapters in this monograph. Dorothy Zinsmeister (Georgia), Nancy Shapiro (Maryland), and Ann Leffler and Norman Jones (Utah) led the efforts in their states with skill and tact. Martin Finkelstein was the best evaluator anyone could ask for, nudging the project leaders in productive directions at many stages of the work. He was ably and energetically assisted by Jennifer Vest Frank in Maryland and Philip Kramer in Utah. Other members of the project advisory team made significant contributions and gave loyal support to the project. AAC&U particularly thanks Teri Hollander in Maryland, Judy Monsas in Georgia, and Teddi Safman in Utah.

High-level staff members of governing and coordinating boards across the country greatly strengthened the project's work by their participation in conferences over the course of the project. Fully half the states sent staff to one or another of these meetings, more than a dozen to all of them. Their enthusiasm for what the project was trying to accomplish was invaluable.

Greater Expectations for Student Transfer was ably directed by Robert Shoenberg, senior fellow at AAC&U, who worked in concert with Andrea Leskes, AAC&U's vice president for education and quality initiatives and director of the Greater Expectations initiative. Kathryn Mueller carried out the enormous task of surveying the general education programs and practices of the fifty states.

AAC&U is most appreciative of the substantial financial support accorded this project by FIPSE and the no less significant personal support of our project officers, Joan Straumanis and Sylvia Crowder, whose good advice and patience has sustained this work over many more years than any of us anticipated. A special thank you also to Michael Ferguson, whose editorial work made this a much better publication than it would otherwise have been.

Greater Expectations for Student Transfer
Seeking Intentionality and the Coherent Curriculum

By Robert Shoenberg

State higher education executive officers (SHEEOs) may sometimes seem intrusive to colleges and universities jealous of their own autonomy, but from a public point of view, governing or coordinating boards—and the university system offices, which often take on similar roles—serve a vital protective role. Nowhere do they better serve the public than in the matter of student transfer. With nearly 60 percent of bachelor's degree recipients having done some substantial portion of their work at more than one institution, efficiency of credit transfer has become a major policy issue. Facilitating student movement among institutions in a state system is essential not only to contain costs for both students and the public, but also to be fair to all involved. The work that the state coordinating and governing agencies have done in recent years in making transfer within their jurisdictions more rational and equitable has helped students substantially and done a great deal for the image of colleges and universities.

However *efficient* and reassuring to students and legislators the hard-won statewide "articulation agreements" may be, the attention they pay to educational *effectiveness* usually ranges from slim to none. For the most part, these agreements focus exclusively on correspondence of subject matter treated in courses. Is it psychology? Is it biology? Is it art history? If it is, then it transfers. Almost never do the rules that govern course articulation attend to the more important question of a correspondence of purposes to which the subject matter is taught. Does the introductory physics course focus primarily on the nature of scientific investigation and the consequences of a scientific mindset on human history and contemporary society? Or does the course take a more parochial view, asking students only to learn and apply to problem sets some basic concepts of the field? Does an introduction to art history deal with the nature of visual representation? Or does it focus primarily on acquainting students with the major artists and typical technical and expressive modes of different periods? As far as most articulation agreements go, these distinctly different approaches to the subject matter are irrelevant. As long as the subject matter is certified as physics or art history, nothing else matters.

Some state systems have become uncomfortable with the notion that, in the interest of fairness and efficiency, it is educationally justifiable to consider as equivalent any courses that deal with similar subject matter. Some institutions that have distinctive and purposefully designed programs bristle at the notion that they must accept in transfer any course with subject matter that corresponds to theirs. They feel that the coherence of their program and the meaning of their degree are subverted by having to accept courses in transfer that are not congruent with their concept of baccalaureate education. Conversely, educationally innovative institutions and their students are angered by the difficulties in transferring courses whose subject matter is interdisciplinary or "different" in some other ways. Any community college that tries to mount a general education program that is not "plain vanilla" is asking for trouble with getting its students' courses transferred.

> The scandal of prevailing articulation practices is that they define a system devoid of a sense of educational purpose.

Statewide articulation agreements do not by and large address these issues. State policy guidelines are the product of extensive negotiation among many parties, each with its own interests to protect, brokered by the higher education governing or coordinating board. Boards and institutions are usually acting under legislative directive or the threat of such a directive to get their transfer policies in order and stop costing students and the state time and money. The legislatures and the public they represent cannot be bothered by such subtle matters as equivalence of educational purpose. Some of a system's campuses may not want to be held to any such equivalence because corporately and in the persons of individual faculty members they wish, as a general principle, to protect their autonomy. And so they settle on the lowest-common-denominator standard, which is subject matter equivalence.

The principal advantage to creating a sieve with such a large mesh is that almost nothing gets screened out. Community colleges do not have to worry so much that their courses won't transfer to particular institutions. Receiving institutions spend much less time on evaluating transcripts. Disputes almost never arise or are quickly resolved. For example, a state-level committee in Maryland created to hear student appeals on credit transfer has never had to meet.

The scandal of prevailing articulation practices is that they define a system devoid of a sense of educational purpose. The emphasis is entirely on efficiency. Students are offered no help in developing a sense of why they are taking courses other than a requirement that they study certain subject matters. Their advisers have trouble answering students' perennial question, "Why do I have to take this course?"

The Aims of Education

This publication is about the ways in which a few states have tried to create conditions that provide some coherent answers to questions about goals for students' general education as part of thoughtful, educationally sound statewide transfer policies. Because they are working on such a large scale and with many institutions jealous of their autonomy, these statewide agencies and systems, working through faculty committees, have had to provide rather general answers. To provide even these general answers has taken a great deal of time. But it is no small accomplishment to have reached any consensus about purposes.

In all cases, these statements of educational purpose and the more detailed regulations that accompany them are focused on general education. The states whose stories are told in this report have laid out statements of purpose for the preexisting statewide general education requirements and in some cases have established guidelines and processes for approval of individual courses or whole programs meeting these requirements. As their individual stories will show, each state has taken a different route to its goals. Together, their stories provide a set of good models for others to follow.

This introductory essay lays out the rationale for emulating the purposes of these states in creating statements of intention for their general education requirements and giving them a sense of coherence. It also provides an overview of practice nationwide with regard to general education at the state level and sketches out the practices of some of the states that have advanced the farthest toward the goals of intentionality and coherence.

Some of the work described in the following pages has gone on in the context of Greater Expectations for Student Transfer, an Association of American Colleges and Universities (AAC&U) project supported by a grant from the Fund for the Improvement of Postsecondary Education (FIPSE). As part of this project, state-level agencies in Georgia, Maryland, and Utah have worked with AAC&U over six years to identify the educational purposes of their preexisting statewide requirements, specify learning outcomes implicit in their requirements, and make these purposes clear to all faculty members teaching courses that meet those requirements. The second part of this publication tells their stories, the lessons from which are summarized in the concluding chapter by the project evaluator, Martin Finkelstein.

Intentionality and Coherence

A competent college curriculum, like any estimable work of human design, must have a clear sense of purpose and elements that cohere around its stated intentions. Many observers of higher education are troubled that so many baccalaureate curricula, whether of institutions as a whole or individual programs within them, fail to pass the test of intentionality and coherence. General education programs in particular are notorious for their lack of clearly stated and understood purpose and the vague relationship, in practice if not in theory, of individual courses to the purported goals of the program.

This lack of clarity of both ends and means is confusing to students. Faced with a set of course requirements whose purpose is not made clear to them, students frequently see general education courses as evils necessary to endure, as obligations to be "gotten out of the way" before getting on to their majors. Often their advisers, themselves lacking a clear understanding of general education programs, are of little help.

These problems of purpose and effectiveness are magnified when students complete their general education requirements at multiple institutions. Even if the public institutions in a particular state have a common general education course requirement (as in Georgia or New York), there is no guarantee that the courses that meet a requirement will be taught to the same ends. Thus students encounter a hodgepodge of courses whose place in their educations is undefined and whose intended relationship to each other is unspecified. Individual courses may be interesting, but the program as a whole appears inconsequential. Having no basis in curricular design on which to build a coherent program for themselves, students see the whole as no more than the sum of the parts, trees but no forest.

Weak to nonexistent connection between general education and the major program further exacerbates the problem. Most colleges and universities treat these two parts of the baccalaureate program as separate entities rather than as intertwined parts of a liberal education. Even if a given institution does organize its majors to further the broad purposes of liberal learning, a student transferring to that institution after completing the general education program at another one may not bring an educational experience that meshes with that of the more purposeful receiving institution. In addition to having some difficulty in completing the more integrated program, the student has gotten a less coherent education.

Perhaps because students do not characteristically give much thought to the matter, they do not often voice concerns about a lack of coherence as such. But their questioning of the reasons for requirements and the burdensomeness of studying particular subject matters is a manifestation of such concerns, however imperfectly articulated. In general, they appear to assume that the design of their majors, especially in professional fields, has a logic, if only to cover those areas of knowledge and skill they need to begin practice in an occupational field or go on to further study. They also assume that they will be prepared in earlier courses to undertake the work of later ones.

Students in most majors readily perceive at least the coherence provided by coverage and progression.[1] General education programs have no such logic, unless one considers distribution requirements a form of coverage. Thus students tend to see distribution requirements as a fact of life, a set of mutually exclusive tasks they must complete satisfactorily. They do not spend much time worrying about the conceptual and organizational principles that govern them, but simply get on with the task of doing what they must do.

Yet when AAC&U invited college juniors and seniors from different regions of the country to discuss the aims of liberal education, many of these students forcefully volunteered their view that while the goals of general education are good ones, their own experience with general education did not live up to the ideal (Hart Research Associates 2004 and 2005). Many of the college students with whom AAC&U spoke felt that their general education courses were completely disconnected from their majors. Some of the students also expressed the view that their general education classes had not taught them anything they hadn't already learned in high school. Whether the students inquire about purposes or not, the findings of these focus groups indicate clear dissatisfaction with general education on the part of advanced college students in four very different regions of the country and at a wide array of schools.

For a group of people whose professional lives are devoted to organizing the data of the phenomenal world and establishing explanatory principles for everything, professors often do a poor job of bringing their educational principles to the level of consciousness and helping students see their value. If the purpose of scholarship is to make coherent sense of the world, why should that purpose be suspended in the case of teaching students about their education? Why should E. M. Forster's well-known dictum, "Only connect," not be brought to bear on college studies?

As AAC&U argues in the *Greater Expectations* report, for students to become intentional learners, colleges and universities must educate them to be "integrative thinkers who can see connections in seemingly disparate information" (2002, 21). Teaching students how to make sense of their baccalaureate programs, how to see the connections, is not simply a matter of practicing what we preach. Students benefit from

---

[1] The common exceptions are social science and humanities majors, which are often deliberately diffuse and unstructured.

understanding what we ask them to do as part of an encompassing logical structure that has purpose. The "shopping mall curriculum" of colleges and universities results in such a scattered educational experience that, cynically viewed, a baccalaureate education appears to be no more than the accumulation of an arbitrarily set number of courses or credit hours. The whole is no more than the sum of the parts—or less if the work of some courses appears so inconsequential that it is promptly forgotten.

If colleges and universities were true to their purposes, students would be able to experience the joy of seeing the growth of their capacities and understandings along clearly articulated pathways of intellectual maturation. They would understand their education as more than an accumulation of course credits. They would also be able to see a baccalaureate education as promoting growth in their capacities to understand, inquire, connect, apply, and empathize. They would have experience using these capacities to deal with complex problems.

Creating such coherence for transfer students (as for students who complete all their baccalaureate work at a single institution) is essential. With transfer students now constituting the majority of graduates of four-year institutions, states are the only possible guarantors of the integrity and coherence of a baccalaureate degree so defined. Their policy statements can appropriately speak to outcomes couched in those terms without infringing on the autonomy of institutions any more than the regional accrediting institutions do.

Indeed, the regional accrediting associations, representing groups of institutions among which students are most likely to transfer, might assist in the transfer process by establishing expectations of programmatic coherence within their regions in addition to individual institutions. They do, however, lack a cross-institutional reach or access to system-wide policies. Their current emphasis on outcomes assessment has already had an especially valuable effect in getting institutions to define their academic goals for students, but that stress affects only individual institutions, not state systems. On the other hand, as AAC&U documented in *Taking Responsibility for the Quality of the Baccalaureate Degree* (2004), several of the accrediting associations for professional programs (e.g., in engineering, nursing, and business) have in recent years made substantial contributions to programmatic coherence across institutions by changing the way in which they state their overarching goals for collegiate programs in their fields and in general education.

The states more successful in establishing common goals and purposes across institutions have adopted a concept of baccalaureate education, and of general education in particular, framed in terms of general intellectual skills rather than specific categories of subject matter. The central elements include

- basic skills acquisition (communication, quantitative reasoning, technology skills, foreign language competence, etc.);

- the nature of different ways of knowing (commonly embodied in "distribution requirements" in sciences, social sciences, humanities, and the arts);
- the competencies and obligations of an educated citizen in a democratic society;
- diversity and the difference that difference makes;
- the interrelatedness of cultures in a global society;
- ethical and moral reasoning.

Translated into language more congruent with students' experience, this conceptualization of the elements of a baccalaureate degree defines a purpose students can understand and accept. For faculty members and institutions this outline of the learning to be acquired in the course of an undergraduate education implies a set of approaches to subject matter within which they have a large degree of freedom. It defines the goals that students are expected to reach and forms a basis for assessment of the outcomes of an undergraduate education. Since both general education and the major can and should consciously contribute to students' achievement of each of these goals, it breaks down the artificial barriers between the two large elements of the undergraduate curriculum.

Were state systems to frame their minimum requirements in this way and faculty members to teach within this framing, they would make it much easier for students to maintain a sense of programmatic coherence as they transfer among institutions. Students would encounter courses with a commonality of purpose regardless of subject matter or institutional curricular differences. They would know what academic experiences to seek out in order to reach the educational goals set for them and upon which they will be assessed. They would find no need to ask, "Why do I have to take this course?"

The Transfer Phenomenon

According to the most recent data from the National Center for Education Statistics (Adelman, Daniel, and Berkovits 2003), 59.2 percent of baccalaureate degree recipients had attended two or more institutions as undergraduates. The majority of these students had earned all their baccalaureate credits from institutions in the same state (68.2 percent of those who attended only two institutions; 47.7 percent of those who attended more than two).

This movement of students is not only from two-year to four-year institutions. While the largest percentage of transfer students follows this pattern (31 percent), 19.1 percent of transfers are between four-year institutions and 20.7 percent between two-year colleges. "Reverse transfer" from four-year to two-year institutions accounts for 14.2 percent of the movement.

Both the numbers and the "swirl" of transfer just outlined fully justify the entrance of state higher education commissions into the arena of baccalaureate purposes on the grounds of enhancing educational quality at the state level. This intervention affects substantial numbers of students whose direction of movement follows multiple patterns with unpredictable consequences for coherence and consistency of purpose.

Transfer Policy and Practice in the Fifty States

AAC&U staff recently completed an informal survey of general education requirements and transfer policies in the fifty states; current information was found for forty-eight, largely through Web sites. In many of the states this information is hard to find, scattered, and conveyed through opaque language. Many people who would benefit from having it, particularly students, would not necessarily know where to look for it—nor would they necessarily understand it if they found it.

The survey revealed an enormous variety of practice with regard to the establishment of general requirements. However, in no state is the requirement organized in terms other than subject matter. The differences lie in how the requirement is rationalized and enforced.

Despite the difficulty in acquiring definitive information, and allowing for some arbitrariness, the states' regulations may be categorized as follows:

- In the largest number of states (twenty-two), the coordinating or governing board has specified a general education requirement that includes both total credits and particular numbers of credits in specific areas that students at all institutions must complete to earn a bachelor's degree.
- In three states with small higher education systems and a single university, these requirements are set by the state university.
- Another nine states have created a general education package which does not have the force of regulation but which, if followed by students, will automatically be accepted in transfer. Most of these states have specified the number and kinds of general education credits that must be included in the package in order to have the program accepted by the receiving institution as meeting all lower-division general education requirements, but individual institutions are free to design other kinds of programs and work out articulation arrangements on their own. In Illinois, Michigan, and Nebraska, institutional acceptance of the transfer package is voluntary, though nearly all receiving institutions participate. In Michigan, the state association of admissions officers and registrars, not the state SHEEO, provided the impetus for the plan and continues to supervise it. In Nebraska and Wyoming, the plan originated with the community colleges and was joined by the four-year institutions.
- Four states have no statewide general education requirements but four-year institutions must consider those who complete the general education program at a two-year college as having satisfied lower-division general education requirements.

- In only ten states is there literally no kind of statewide arrangement for either the design or transfer of a general education program. All of these states have some system of designating course equivalences among all institutions, the most elaborate being Florida's common course numbering system. In this system all courses with the same number, having been reviewed by a statewide faculty committee, are considered equivalent for transfer purposes. Some of the SHEEOs in these states with no common general requirement have promulgated a general education "pattern" reflecting the points of commonality among general education programs at the state's four-year institutions. These artificial programs in essence say to students, "If you take this set of courses it will meet most of the general education requirements at most receiving institutions." None of these ten states, however, makes any effort to regulate either the extent of general education programs or the distribution of general education courses.

All states, then, maintain some listing of courses transferable as meeting general education requirements. All but ten states have some arrangement for transfer of general education packages among all public institutions in the system; the remaining states leave it up to individual institutions to work out transfer arrangements. The minimum size of those packages is specified in thirty-six states. The minimum number of credits required ranges from thirty to sixty, with one large group clustering around thirty-two and another around forty. General education requirements of more than forty-two credits are outliers in the pattern.

The composition of the statewide general education programs has a remarkable consistency. All require one or two writing courses, a college-level mathematics course, and some distribution of courses among the major domains of knowledge. The modal pattern is two courses each in the arts, humanities, sciences, and social sciences. Many states require more than the thirty to thirty-three hours that this pattern implies.

Only seventeen states require study in additional areas or specify particular intellectual skills that must be addressed in the process of completing these requirements. In the intellectual skills category, four states specify "critical thinking," three "ethical reasoning," and one "lifelong understanding and development." Also in the "skills" category, five states require a course in oral communication and five require one in technology. Colorado requires specific attention to the skills of critical reading in the context of the subject matter courses.

Two areas that have more recently entered the general education canon, diversity in American society and global awareness, are required elements in general education in five states each. Three of these states require attention to both.

Apart from the ubiquitous system of distribution requirements, no particular subject matter seems to be required with much frequency. Three states specify history rather than including it in the humanities or social sciences. Economics or political science is specified in two states while a course in one of these or American history constitutes Utah's unique "American institutions" requirement. Subjects of study required in a single state include the environment (Minnesota), philosophy (Connecticut), foreign language (New York), and physical education (Tennessee). Ohio requires an interdisciplinary course.

The fact that only the Ohio transfer package makes specific reference to interdisciplinary work illustrates a defining characteristic of these programs: their orientation toward individual subject matters as represented by traditional academic departments. To put it bluntly, these general education transfer programs are "plain vanilla" and do not represent or advance the innovative developments in general education of recent years. These transfer programs are designed to reflect the lowest common denominator of general education programs that are actually in place at most institutions, even though individual institutions may have more complex, extensive, and imaginative general requirements. Because they were the product of compromise among the many parties sitting at the table when the transfer policy was hammered out, they were structured to require the least adjustment possible at any institution. Equally important to their designers, they had to create the fewest problems possible for students transferring from two-year to four-year institutions and make it convenient for the two-year institutions' general education programs to transfer intact to four-year institutions. Interdisciplinary or other requirements not readily identifiable with the standard structure of departments have the potential for creating awkwardness.

Thus the transfer packages constrain curricular innovation. If two-year institutions create distinctive general education offerings they run the risk that the courses will not be approved for transfer. The receiving institutions cannot hold transfer students to any unique lower-division requirements or program structures that they create for their "native" students. Transcript auditors, in honoring articulation agreements, must align the two-year college transfer's standard program with the receiving institution's differently structured requirements in any way they can, which sometimes produces bizarre assignments of equivalence.

Despite the fact that nearly all states maintain a list of courses at each campus that meet statewide requirements, only fourteen maintain a system of state-level review either for all the courses placed on the list or for general education programs as a whole. Three states (Arizona, Missouri, Ohio) review programs. The remaining states do their vetting at the course level. Interestingly, only six of the states that have clear statements of educational intentions for general education also engage in course or program approval. The others specify intentions but do not enforce them. The eight states that have system-level approval processes but no clear statements of intention appear to be looking only at whether the course or program corresponds to the subject matter category.

Innovation and distinctiveness are better encouraged in those states that are specific about the intentions of the statewide requirements. In these jurisdictions, those who are auditing transcripts can use the spirit of the regulations to determine equivalences rather than feeling constrained by the letter of law. The problem is that only ten states—Colorado, Georgia, Hawaii, Illinois, Maryland, Minnesota, Missouri, New York, Texas, and Utah—have spelled out in any detail the intentions of each of their requirements. In the other states, any course with an appropriate subject matter will do, even if the approved courses differ widely in what students are actually expected to learn.

The Role of Faculty

In the ten states that have made intentions clear, the opportunity for students to experience consistency of purpose across institutions is enhanced, but only if instructors at the individual institutions in the system are responsive to those statements of intention. The evidence, however, is that the writ of SHEEOs does not, in this matter, extend very far. Interviews with undergraduate program administrators and faculty at both two-year and four-year institutions in states with some of the strongest system-level statements of general education purposes reveal that faculty members and academic advisers are unevenly aware of discussions that have gone on and determinations that have been made at the state level. Some campus general education programs, department general education offerings, and individual faculty practices reflect the awareness and experience faculty members have gained at state-level conferences or by serving as members of course and program approval panels. However, the institutional impact of individual faculty members' experiences beyond the campus is highly variable and haphazard. Translation from the clarity and consistency of state-level determinations to campus practice is quite uneven.

> Only ten states have spelled out in any detail the intentions of each of their requirements.

Even in a state with a strong system of general education course approval at the system level, most instructors who teach general education courses remain unaware of the program's overarching expectations. In many cases, dean- and provost-level administrators tend to mediate the process of gaining course approval, involving classroom instructors only as necessary. Shielding the faculty from the annoyance of bureaucratic processes has undeniable advantages in terms of convenience, consistency, and time saving, but it short circuits the education of instructors about the system's intentions for general education.

Faculty awareness of program and course purposes gets support from a seemingly unrelated set of activities: conversations between college and high school instructors. These conversations are often sponsored by a formal "K–16 program," active in several states, the purpose of which is to create a seamless system of education from preschool programs through the baccalaureate degree (see, for example, the case of Maryland in chapter 4). Through these programs, substantial numbers of secondary school and college instructors have been successful in specifying the skills and knowledge that students should have acquired at each level. College faculty participation has led to important clarification of the intentions of collegiate programs and levels of expectation, particularly in English composition and mathematics, which has in turn led to greater consistency of purpose in those fields.

Having such generally accepted, widely propagated standards is particularly important in general education programs in which much of the teaching is done by non-tenure-track instructors who come and go with great frequency. Most such instructors—graduate students, adjuncts, lecturers—get only limited orientation and training for their work. Having clear statements of purposes and standards as a point of reference is immensely helpful to all.

Examples of State Practices

As we have seen, most statewide general education transfer policies are designed to maximize transfer of academic credit for students moving among institutions in the state system. They are meant to be efficient and convenient and to reduce uncertainty. Some states have tried to introduce into this process a broad statement of educational purpose for their general requirements. These statements are intended to make general education somewhat more coherent for students moving from one institution to another. Some specific examples of policies and practices in these states, briefly summarized, will illustrate both the possibilities and the difficulties of more aggressive state efforts to create intentionality and coherence in general education. Fuller stories of such efforts are contained in the detailed accounts of activities in Georgia, Maryland, and Utah in the following chapters.

Colorado

Colorado's program of "state-guaranteed student transfer" is characterized by state-level approval of individual general education courses based on well-defined criteria. Committees drawn from faculty at both two-year and four-year institutions meet annually to approve courses submitted for guaranteed transfer status in each of five "content areas" (communication, arts and humanities, mathematics, natural and physical sciences, and social and behavioral sciences) and five "competency areas" (critical thinking, written communication, technology, reading, and mathematics). The 2001 act of the state legislature that occasioned development of this structure actually specifies only the competencies that a general education program is designed to foster. A traditional general education program of thirty-five to thirty-seven hours in the five content areas was defined through a statewide faculty conference as a vehicle by means of which the competencies are to be achieved through these content area courses. This combination of content area courses with specific expectations of attention to the competencies creates an extensive "across-the-curriculum" structure. (See the sidebar for an example of criteria for critical thinking competency.)

The Colorado Commission on Higher Education (CCHE) is responsible for administering the course approval process and maintaining the list of guaranteed transfer courses. The "GE-25 Committee," made up of representatives of each public institution in the state, advises CCHE on policy and process. Course approval rests with large faculty committees in each content area. In the first two years of program operation, several hundred courses have been approved.

Institutions do not have to nominate courses for guaranteed transfer approval, though all have nominated some. Colleges that have many students transferring, especially the community colleges, provide the greatest benefit to students by getting as many courses as possible approved, while primarily receiving institutions feel less

Criteria for Critical Thinking Competency in Colorado

Guiding Principle: The goal of instruction in "critical thinking" is to help students become capable of critical and open-minded questioning and reasoning. An understanding of argument is central to critical thinking.

Definition: Critical Thinking Competency
Ability to examine issues and ideas and to identify good and bad reasoning in a variety of fields with differing assumptions, contents, and methods.

Criteria
1. Information Acquisition
   - Identify questions, problems, and arguments.
   - Differentiate questions, problems, and arguments.
2. Application
   - Evaluate the appropriateness of various methods of reasoning and verification.
   - State position or hypothesis, give reasons to support it and state its limitations.
3. Analysis
   - Identify stated and unstated assumptions.
   - Assess stated and unstated assumptions.
   - Critically compare different points of view.
4. Synthesis
   - Formulate questions and problems.
   - Construct and develop cogent arguments.
   - Articulate reasoned judgments.
5. Communication
   - Discuss alternative points of view.
   - Defend or criticize a point of view in view of available evidence.
6. Evaluation
   - Evaluate the quality of evidence and reasoning.
   - Draw an appropriate conclusion.

The above bullets represent the full spectrum of criteria that may define this competency. For the purposes of qualifying as a state-guaranteed general education course that requires this competency, the institution must demonstrate that the course substantively addresses most, not necessarily all, of the stated criteria.

Source: Colorado Commission on Higher Education.

urgency to nominate courses. Some of the larger universities, which characteristically teach general education courses through large lectures, have been reluctant to nominate these courses because they cannot meet the requirement that they include work in written communication.

On the other hand, the state-supported community colleges and some that are locally supported have been quick to respond. These institutions have a common course numbering system, so all community college courses with a common number are, at least in theory, taught to the same ends. Thus Colorado has a community college general education program with a common set of intentions across institutions, while four-year institutions may or may not have programs that share these intentions.

The major problem has been approval of unique and interdisciplinary courses, which, for whatever reasons, the state has been uncertain how to handle. Absence of favorable action on these courses has been another reason for the four-year institutions' tardiness in nominating courses. Some of the more interesting curricular experiments, particularly at community colleges, may be damped out if the approval process cannot deal with these courses. Honors programs, which characteristically include interdisciplinary work, may also suffer. If the exceptions to common practice—and they are many—cannot gain approval for guaranteed transfer, the result may be a statewide general education program with homogenized content rather than one with a uniformity of purpose realized in a wide variety of ways.

These concerns do not, however, diminish the considerable accomplishment of Colorado in developing a clear statement of general education purposes that integrally addresses both content and competencies. The clearly stated criteria for course approval specify the ends to which a course in a particular area is to be taught without restricting either the means or the specific content of the course. If these specifications can be rendered as statements of purpose clear to students, students should have no confusion about the purposes of general education no matter where they may find themselves in the system.

Illinois has a quite similar program, the Illinois Articulation Initiative (IAI), which was implemented in 1998. It served as the principal model for the Colorado's Guaranteed Transfer Program. Participation in the IAI is entirely voluntary, but more than 110 institutions, public, private, and proprietary, participate. The thirty-seven- to forty-one-credit General Education Core Curriculum package, as part of an associate degree, is recognized by all participating institutions as meeting "the receiving institution's all-campus, lower-division general education requirement for the baccalaureate degree."

As of summer 2003, twenty thousand courses in the state had been approved by five general education panels and twenty-seven major field panels, each composed of twenty-one faculty members representing all the sectors plus three transfer specialists and a community college administrator.

Courses proposed for approval by the institutions are reviewed for "comparability in scope, quality, and intellectual rigor." Course descriptions, many couched in terms of student learning outcomes, and panel "decision rules" are important factors in determining approval. For example, certification of the two-course writing sequence requires documentation of multisource writing with a minimum of 2,500 words. Oral communication courses must include three "substantial" speeches, defined as at least five minutes in length.

Missouri

Missouri is one of only two states, **Ohio** being the other, that approves *programs* rather than courses at the state level. Both states specify a transfer "module" of a minimum number of hours (forty-two credits in Missouri, thirty-six to forty in Ohio) and certain general content. Missouri's program superimposes a structure of four knowledge areas (humanities and fine arts, social and behavioral sciences, natural sciences, and mathematics) on four skill areas (communicating, higher-order thinking, managing information, and valuing). For each knowledge and skill area the program prescribes goals and offers illustrative competencies. Each institution is free to design its own program aligned with these goals and competencies.

Campuses seeking approval for their programs post them on the Web for review by the other institutions. In addition to describing their general education programs in the usual ways, institutions must complete a "general education reporting matrix" or "alignment analysis" that shows the ways in which the expected outcomes will be realized. They are guided in this effort by the statewide general education policy, which includes a rationale for general education and for each of the competency and content areas, the state-level goal for each area, and "suggested competencies" toward which courses in each area might be directed.

Other institutions in the state may then comment on the program, indicating any ways in which it may be unacceptable for block transfer. After making whatever changes it deems appropriate, the offering institution notifies the coordinating board that it is implementing the program. Potential receiving institutions which believe the program is still inadequate may appeal the practices and policies of another institution, though in practice they are reluctant to do so formally.

Students who have completed the block may then transfer it to the general education program at the receiving institution. If students have not completed the entire block at their original institution, they are subject to the usual course-by-course evaluation of credits. The receiving institution may impose additional general requirements for transfer students if they are also required for their own native students.

The process by which the Missouri Coordinating Board for Higher Education brought this system into being might serve as a model for all states wishing to gain real commitment to statewide commonality of intention for general education and coherence of student programs. A state-level general education steering committee conducted studies and surveys to identify the nature and extent of existing problems with general education and transfer, thus making a convincing case for action. The committee maintained a commitment to faculty control of curriculum and institutional autonomy in curricular design, and its processes included extensive opportunity for comment and revision. The result has been unusually good reception of the new regulations and their means of implementation.

At least until budget problems intervened, the coordinating board sponsored an annual one-day conference on general education for faculty and academic administrators on transfer articulation issues. Issues surrounding general education policy and practices were a major component of the conference. About six hundred people attended each of these meetings, assuring that large numbers of faculty members have a good acquaintance with statewide policy.

Utah

Remarkably, Utah's efforts to rationalize general education requirements at the state's nine public institutions came from a group of faculty members. Formed by leadership from Utah State University and soon allied with the state's board of regents, the Regents' Task Force on General Education has worked for eight years to create a common sense of purpose for general education throughout Utah.

The main vehicle for the task force's work has been a series of annual "What Is an Educated Person?" conferences. These meetings, typically attended by about 120 faculty members and academic administrators, have been the occasion for discussing the purposes of general education and developing statements of the characteristics that courses in each category should exhibit. These statements have been developed for each of the requirements mandated by the regents: five distribution categories (natural sciences and physical sciences get separate attention), mathematics, writing, technology, and American institutions. The last is a requirement, unique to Utah, for a course in American history, politics, or economics.

In response to a threatened legislative requirement to assess general education outcomes by means of a standardized test, the Regents' Task Force was able to organize a faculty-developed assessment in writing, mathematics, and American institutions. The assessment was conducted once with encouragingly positive results, but lack of funds has prevented additional administrations of the instruments and further development of the assessment strategy.

The task force chose to operate in ways that encourage faculty members to pay attention to general education purposes rather than working toward imposition of state regulations and course or program approval processes. Such a strategy is more compatible with faculty culture and has a chance of working in a state with Utah's small higher education system. The board of regents and organizations within the state's business community have been quite supportive. The problem, however, remains getting the attention of enough faculty members to have a noticeable effect on the way in which general education courses are conceived and taught and how students are informed and advised. Though progress is slow, project leaders can see positive results from this continuing effort.

Georgia

If the faculty-led efforts in Utah represent a "bottom-up" process of dealing with general education statewide, Georgia is characteristic of a "top-down" approach. Here the initiative originated with the board of regents and specifically with the system chancellor. Coincident with a calendar conversion from quarters to semesters, the regents established a general education core curriculum and course numbering system common to all thirty-four campuses in the University System of Georgia, which includes both two- and four-year institutions.[2]

These changes were accompanied by the creation of a structure of statewide faculty committees to tend to the common elements of the system curriculum. Academic Advisory Committees in each discipline are made up of one faculty member from each campus at which the field is represented. Fourteen of these committees, originally charged with studying the curricula and major programs at each campus, have been engaged with the new core through a charge to develop general learning outcomes for courses commonly taught in the core. The Council on General Education, which originally operated in a program monitoring role, has taken up the task of establishing criteria for courses to meet core curriculum requirements.

As in other states that have addressed the intentionality of general requirements, this process constitutes rationalization after the fact. In Georgia, however, large numbers of campus faculty members are engaged in thinking through the intentions of the core requirements and developing common outcomes and criteria for approval of courses that meet the requirements. Through these many representatives and through an annual statewide conference on general education, faculty members on the campuses are kept sensitive to core curriculum purposes. Transfer advisers on each campus form a parallel network of informed individuals who are in direct contact with students. A statewide, Web-based advising program directed at students provides an additional source of information about program intentions and purposes.

Maryland

While the Maryland SHEEO organization, the Maryland Higher Education Commission, has a formal policy on course transfer, the major state initiative to define the intentions of general requirements and general education outcomes has been assumed by the University System of Maryland (USM). The system, which includes eleven of the thirteen four-year public institutions in the state but none of the two-year colleges, has used as its main mechanism for comprehensive involvement a group called the Intersegmental

---

[2] The technical colleges formed a separate system at the time the core curriculum was introduced but have since come under the authority of the regents and have adopted the system's core.

Chief Academic Officers (ICAO). Understanding that a host of academic policies requires the active awareness and participation of all public institutions, this group meets every other month to consider a range of issues involved in the movement of students among institutions and to establish and hear reports from groups created to address these issues. Attendees are either the assistant or associate CAOs who deal with undergraduate curriculum and academic regulations or the CAOs themselves.

The work of this group has been substantially influenced by a particularly active K–16 initiative. Continuing discussions among university faculty and high school teachers in all major college preparatory subjects have led to careful review of typical first-year undergraduate requirements, particularly the purposes of those requirements. Discussions about the nature of the first college-level courses in mathematics have been particularly intense and have resulted in statewide agreement on the purposes of different sorts of courses, including those focused on quantitative literacy. The work includes broad curriculum frameworks and examples of the kinds of problems students completing those courses should be expected to solve. Similarly, English composition program leaders have created and promulgated a document entitled "Standards of a 'C' Paper." This statement describes the attributes that student writing should exhibit in order to be acceptable.

The work of the mathematics group, while begun under the auspices of the K–16 program, was produced as part of an ICAO initiative to establish common sets of standards, goals, and learning outcomes for several kinds of courses commonly used to fulfill general education requirements: physical sciences, biological sciences, fine and performing arts, and English literature, in addition to mathematics. A highly developed version of this kind of work has arisen from successful efforts to implement an associate of arts in teaching (AAT) degree program in the community colleges.

The AAT degree, created partly as a response to the K–16 program mandate to improve teacher preparation, constitutes the first two years of a teacher education program. Students completing this program may transfer automatically to the third-year program at any of Maryland's four-year institutions. Devising an AAT program for prospective secondary school teachers required agreement on the specific outcomes of instruction in the first two years in each secondary field. Concentrating initially on Spanish, physics, chemistry, and mathematics, teachers of these subjects representing both community colleges and four-year institutions produced full statements of the expected outcomes of the AAT program in each discipline. In addition to outcomes statements, the document suggests indicators of achievement of each outcome, types of assessment that might be used, and useful instructional tools to achieve these results. Thus, for the secondary school AAT at least, strong and clear statewide expectations are in place.

Lessons Learned

Intensive work over several years with state systems in Georgia, Maryland, and Utah, extended interaction with SHEEO academic officers in several other states, and a survey of statewide general education policy and administration in all fifty states reveal a developing trend toward more purposeful action on general education at the state level. SHEEOs and state university systems, having largely won the battle for efficiency of course transfer and fair treatment of students in the process, have begun to turn their attention to the substance of general education requirements and coherence in their realization in the classroom.

Ten states have developed cogent statements of purpose for their requirements and five of them have course or program review processes designed to assure that practice matches policy. Several additional states are moving in this direction. The matter of moving institutions within state systems to some commonality of educational purpose is firmly on the table.

Actually realizing in practice the newly stated intentions of the state requirements is, as this project has revealed, extremely difficult. Most systems are very large and the familiar analogy to the length of time and distance it takes to change the direction of a battleship applies here. Committees of a dozen or more faculty members assembled from across a state can reach agreement about the purposes of various requirements quite readily and with little controversy, no matter how large the group. An implicit consensus exists, and the formulations of that consensus in some AAC&U documents (Schneider and Shoenberg 1998; AAC&U 2002) have provided a useful articulation of it.

But conveying these common understandings for student learning from the few who engage in state-level discussions and are interested in these issues to thousands of faculty members on individual campuses who do not habitually pay attention to such matters is a different story. Faculty members are notoriously protective of their autonomy and are likely to see as unwarranted interference any efforts to suggest, let alone enforce, even broad general principles for the ways they teach their courses. Insisting on the axiomatic principle that people who teach a course that fulfills a requirement have an obligation to teach the course in accordance with the purposes of the requirement is of little avail with people who are used to teaching what they wish without being monitored.

Some of the resistance can be overcome simply by involving as many faculty members as possible in the discussion of purposes. Having such discussions among instructors from across the state reveals many more commonalities than disagreements and enhances the development of general understandings which, even if not formalized, enhance commonality of practice.

Such conversations do not, however, get at the problems of communicating intentions to the many part-time instructors who do the bulk of general education teaching and sustaining the effort year after year as new teachers take up these duties. The move to increasingly large numbers of part-time and temporary full-time instructors, driven by reductions in state funding relative to student enrollment, creates a situation in which the sustained vision of purpose upon which states insist is undermined by funding limitations. States generally have not even formulated policy with regard to the expected orientation and training of these part-time instructors.

Those who would try to create some commonality of purpose across the system must also deal with the jealousy of institutions for their autonomy. As is only appropriate, each college or university has worked through the process of establishing a general education program on its own, developing its own concepts and language and taking advantage of its particular circumstances and points of consensus at the time the program was developed. Although general education programs even at quite disparate institutions tend to bear a family resemblance, colleges and universities love their own offspring best. The appearance that the state wants to impose some uniformity on their programs, even though the program would be affected, if at all, only in the way some subject matters are approached, is often resented.

A more realistic misgiving is the difficulty many state systems have in dealing with interdisciplinary or otherwise unusual courses. Faculty committees looking for comparability of courses tend to look at subject matter rather than at the relationship of the nonstandard course to the purposes of the requirement. Excluding these courses for automatic transfer tends to homogenize the curriculum, to restrict general education programs to the assumptions of an earlier era, even as the frontiers of knowledge become interdisciplinary. Two-year institutions have long been familiar with this problem, with the result that few community colleges have a general education curriculum that is at all imaginative or distinctive. These colleges cannot risk requiring students to take courses that will not transfer readily to any of the many institutions that they may subsequently attend.

Conversely, the four-year institutions plan their general education curricula with the implicit assumption that all their graduates will have completed it. Their programs may have a special internal logic and principle of coherence, may be organized quite differently from the statewide consensus model, or may require upper-division work. How to apply the state model that transfer students bring poses a real problem for them. They know that the majority of their baccalaureate recipients have completed a good part of their education at another institution, but they are troubled by awarding their degrees to students whose educational experience does not have the particular quality they have designed for their native students.

The practical problem is taken off the table in the several states with the policy that a general education program completed at one institution will be considered as satisfying general education requirements at any other institution in the state. All of these states have designated minimum credit-hour requirements for general education and a standard package of the kinds of courses general education programs must include. But as we have seen, only a few states have clearly defined the purposes of these requirements and fewer still review and approve programs for their compliance with these intentions. Thus the programs as a whole may transfer readily from one institution to another, but the work transferred may be very different in nature from what the receiving institution conceives of as characterizing its degree. And of course students who do not complete the entire general education program at their original institution are subject to the vagaries of course-by-course credit transfer.

Institutions and individual faculty members are not the only point of difficulty in implementing an intentional and coherent general education program that works across institutions. Many students are indifferent or oblivious to the value or even the possibility of a program that is more than the sum of the individual courses. Their focus is on earning the degree: they have little concern for the principles of curriculum construction. As far as they are concerned, "Whatever is, is right."

Colleges and universities, let alone state higher education systems, generally do a rather poor job of explaining the logic of what they require. Yes, many make a somewhat extended rationale for their requirements available on their Web pages and in their catalogs. But how many students, frustrated by having to fulfill a particular requirement, think to themselves, "Let's see what the state or the college has to say about this requirement on its Web site?" Freshman seminars, when they are offered, may well spend time on the rationale for the college's requirements, but probably do not present them within a statewide context or one that anticipates eventual transfer.

When we look at the actual state-level requirements, the most notable fact about them is their similarity. All requirements or transfer "patterns" are organized in terms of subject matters and consist mainly or exclusively of the standard writing, mathematics, and distribution courses. Despite the trend in accreditation toward requiring and assessing student learning outcomes, only seventeen states impose any other kind of requirement.

In an effort to respond to more contemporary ideas about the function of general education in developing intellectual capacities, Colorado and Missouri have, as we have seen, created ways of overlaying a structure of general intellectual skills on the standard structure of subject matters. Most of the ten states that have developed statements of purpose for their requirements have rationalized them in terms of their value in acquainting students with the "ways of knowing" of the major domains of knowledge. But only in the rare cases (again Missouri and Colorado, as well as Georgia, Illinois, Maryland, Minnesota, and Utah), where the states have deliberately rethought general education, are requirements couched in terms that would lead students to see them as something other than a requirement to study a range of specific subject matters. Thus the courses that fulfill distribution requirements are not seen in relation to each other as a suite of studies of complementary modes of description, analysis, and assignment of value. In most states, distribution requirements are rationalized, if they are justified at all, only as a way of adding some breadth to students' knowledge, rather than as making a contribution to a complete arsenal of modes of analysis and critical thinking and to students' understanding of the world in which they live.

> The purposes of democracy are hobbled when a college education is conceived primarily as a process of credit accumulation.

Even in the states which have developed coherent statements of intention, the rationales are for the most part rationalizations after the fact. These states have taken the requirements that existed and assigned to them a new or differently designed purpose. This strategy reflects the political need to disturb the existing structure as little as possible, to reflect the lowest-common-denominator structure of general education on the individual campuses. The new definitions are intended to influence the point of view from which existing courses are taught but not to cause the campuses to restructure their general education programs. The states have not, however, established the kinds of methods used by Colorado and Missouri to enforce or at least promote their intentions.

Rather than being critical of states that have not moved to modernize their general education programs, we should be gratified that several have shown some aggressiveness in doing so. Given student and legislative pressure to make transfer of credits as easy as possible and institutions' jealousy for their own ways of doing things, it takes considerable courage and patient effort to focus attention on the purposes and principles of intellectual coherence and garner assent for them. The models cited in this introduction and the more detailed stories told in the following chapters show what can be done, and should encourage other states to follow suit. For in this age of student mobility, the states have a new role in guaranteeing the integrity of degrees, a role that individual institutions are finding more difficult to fulfill.

Even after accomplishing this goal, however, the effort will be incomplete without turning attention to assessing student achievement of the fully defined outcome expectations. Not only individual institutions but state systems of higher education as well face increasing pressure to demonstrate the effects of their instructional programs on students. Finding credible ways to aggregate liberal learning outcomes assessment data at the state level will be difficult, but the effort has begun, in Virginia for example, and must be pursued vigorously.

In these efforts both to define and to assess outcomes, the states may find a strong ally in the regional accrediting associations. These organizations have steadily been increasing the pressure on institutions to engage in meaningful outcomes assessment, and no assessment can be meaningful without a clear statement of goals. Regional accreditors and SHEEOs might do well to reach out to each other.

The ultimate beneficiary of greater intentionality and curricular coherence is American society. The purposes of democracy are hobbled when a college education is conceived primarily as a process of credit accumulation. College graduates who know how to make effective life choices, understand and function well in a diverse national and world society, and contribute to their communities are essential to sustaining our democracy. State higher education systems can help focus baccalaureate education on those kinds of goals and advocate for them not only among the institutions over which they have jurisdiction, but also with state legislatures and the public. They can help students rightly understand what their undergraduate education is about and push institutions toward making those common understandings the real underpinning of their instructional programs. As these organizations are charged with seeing the systems they oversee as a whole, so they might play an aggressive role in helping students to understand their education as a whole. They can be the force that insists to students and their colleges, "Only connect."

References

Adelman, C., B. Daniel, and I. Berkovits. 2003. *Postsecondary attainment, attendance, curriculum and performance: Selected results from the NELS: 88/2000 postsecondary education transcript study (PETS), 2000.* Washington, DC: National Center for Education Statistics.

Association of American Colleges and Universities. 2002. *Greater expectations: A new vision for learning as a nation goes to college.* Washington, DC: Association of American Colleges and Universities.

———. 2004. *Taking responsibility for the quality of the baccalaureate degree.* Washington, DC: Association of American Colleges and Universities.

Peter D. Hart Research Associates. 2004. Key findings from focus groups among college students and college-bound high school students. www.aacu.org/advocacy/pdfs/HartFocusGroupResearchReport.pdf

Peter D. Hart Research Associates. 2005. Key findings from focus groups among college students and college-bound high school students in Wisconsin. www.aacu.org/advocacy/pdfs/QualitativeResearchWI.pdf

Schneider, C. G., and R. Shoenberg. 1998. *Contemporary understandings of liberal education.* Washington, DC: Association of American Colleges and Universities.

Faculty Collaboration and Statewide General Education Reform
The Case of Utah

By Ann Leffler, Philip I. Kramer, Norman L. Jones, and Phyllis Safman

If reforming campus general education is like moving a graveyard, then conducting system-wide reform is like levitating one. In the Winter 2000 issue of *Peer Review*, Robert Shoenberg cogently explained that system-wide general education reform is fraught with potential conflicts. And yet in the Utah System of Higher Education, faculty have become accustomed to, even enthusiastic about, collaborating across institutional and disciplinary boundaries to improve general education. Despite the professoriate's customary loyalties to individual institutions and disciplines, faculties in Utah have found it worthwhile to think statewide about general education goals.

Why Consider Statewide Collaboration?

General education reform should be approached at the state level as well as locally. Taking this approach, however, requires many faculty to assume new identities. They must define themselves as *general education* faculty, not just faculty in particular disciplines; as *statewide* faculty, not just members of individual departments and institutions; and, most importantly, as *civic intellectuals*—public leaders—not just hapless punch dolls knocked down by hostile external forces, perpetually bouncing back to the hopeless task of standing up long enough actually to educate people.

Why should faculty do this? In this volume, both Shoenberg and Finkelstein report that an increasing number of students transfer between institutions. That growth may expand even more with transfers into and out of e-classes. There are also transfers from high school courses in which some students acquire as many as two years of college credit via advanced placement or dual enrollment. And there are students who do more than one of these things. In the past, colleges considered their reputable students "homegrown." A stigma attached to the rest. As a result, the somewhat seedy issue of articulation was either not practiced openly (institutions simply rejected outside courses) or was done laboriously, institution by institution and course by course.

Increasingly, transfer demographics and the accompanying political pressures discourage such snobbery, at least with respect to general education articulation. Too often what this means, however, is that faculty lose ownership of articulation. General education courses are articulated wholesale via statewide mechanical agreements that reflect ease of implementation rather than educational purposefulness. (The same may one day be true for curricula in the majors.) Every course at one institution becomes equivalent, usually because of a common course number or name, to every other such course at another institution. Make no mistake: when a transfer student is given three credits for a Psychology 101 course because the same name and number exist at that student's new school, the two courses have just been made equivalent. When a university looks at a transfer transcript, sees Biology 101 on it, and checks off a student's life sciences requirement, it is allowing the name and number to stand in for whatever educational purpose that requirement was intended to address.

> When general education is changed from without and faculty believe they have lost ownership, they may retreat into areas of the curriculum they feel they still control—the major and graduate education—or they may ignore the external mandates.

We do not believe that educational purposefulness and transfer are antonyms. Rather, faculty must lead statewide collaborations to create larger visions of educational purpose. Why the faculty? On other political issues, it is a truism that change requires mobilizing key constituencies. This is true in academe too. Within the culture of faculty governance that has shaped American higher education for many decades, the faculty owns the curriculum. Certainly outside pressures like legislative mandates are a perennial possibility; certainly over time cultural forces shape and change the American classroom. But in the short term—which is the time frame desired for general education reform—what happens in individual classrooms largely reflects the desires of individual teachers. To reform general education, the faculty must be mobilized. When general education is changed from without and faculty believe they have lost ownership, they may retreat into areas of the curriculum they feel they still control—the major and graduate education—or they may ignore the external mandates. So if offering transfer students purposeful general education is a goal, faculty must collaborate across institutions to shape and own the new approach. This leads us to what has happened in Utah.

The Utah Approach

The catalyst for Utah's system-wide collaboration to reform general education is the Regents' Task Force on General Education. This task force was originally convened in 1992 by Utah's chief academic officers (CAOs) through the Utah System of Higher Education. It was a typical system-based ad hoc group. Its specific charge was very different from and much more modest than to reform general education: it was convened to evaluate a proposal by one campus for televised general education courses. The proposed use of television as a medium of instruction raised questions about the worth of what might be offered there. But when the task force tackled this issue, it was immediately evident that the system had no way of defining "worth." This realization led to explorations of what general education was accomplishing statewide, and what it could accomplish. A snowball effect ensued, in which success at one venture led to explorations in another. Since 1992, the task force has been charged by Utah's chief academic officers and the regents with a wide range of work involving statewide collaboration on general education. In addition, it has adopted the informal mission of serving as a key intellectual "meeting place" where faculty can exchange information and ideas about what is happening on each campus, and develop a shared perspective on curricular issues. Itself an example of faculty ownership, the task force also proselytizes for faculty ownership of issues ranging from general education to outcomes assessment.

Statewide Collaboration on General Education Goals

Although convened to address the modest issue of televised courses, once together, faculty representatives to the task force from Utah's six public four-year and three two-year schools quickly began doing what faculty do when they get a chance to think beyond local and disciplinary borders: they began exploring common goals. This eventually raised the possibility of seeking goals that transcended individual institutions. Importantly, in this process, the task force wanted to support distinctive faculty voices and campus missions. How could both similarity and difference be protected? The task force started with the question "What is an educated person?" and followed it to explore whether statewide faculty shared pedagogical values—we sought common goals, not common courses—sufficiently to develop a mutual vision of general education. How much agreement was there about the core skills faculty want their students to develop?

Four years, many conversations, and—naturally—many subcommittees later, the task force agreed on a set of joint competencies in nine general education areas: quantitative literacy, writing, the social sciences, the humanities, the life sciences, the fine arts, the physical sciences, technology and computers, and (because it is a course mandated by the legislature) American institutions.

These are meant to represent minimum, not maximum, standards; they are meant to permit institutions great flexibility in how they are "packaged" for curriculum inclusion; and, we say with some trepidation, they are meant to be assessable at both entry and exit levels.

Statewide Collaboration on the Purposes of Education

The task force also decided that public conversations about higher education would be elevated beyond misunderstanding and cynicism only if we could remind the public—and ourselves—of the goals of higher learning. To this end, we began working with an organization of chief executive officers from some of Utah's largest corporations. Their answers to "What is an educated person?" have proved both enlightening and politically useful. For instance, they insisted that students have a well-rounded general education that teaches them communication skills, exposes them to cultural diversity, and fosters various other educational outcomes that faculty sometimes fear are devalued outside academe.

With enthusiastic support from the commissioner of higher education and the chief academic officers, we also convened a regional conference titled "What Is an Educated Person?" The conference format mixed representatives from all the regional institutions, including private ones like Westminster College and Brigham Young University, and some Idaho schools that transfer large numbers of students to Utah, with business and political leaders. This first conference was so successful that seven more have followed. Topics of the second through fourth conferences involved assessment (discussed below), while the fifth conference, titled "It's Not Your Grandparents' Gen Ed Anymore," covered technological and other changes in pedagogies and content, changes in the ways general education faculty respond to those changes, and the changing connections between high school and the general education curriculum. The sixth conference focused on how students learn and explored patterns of student transfer, time to graduation, and curricular problems in light of the Association of American Colleges and Universities' 2002 *Greater Expectations* report. The most recent conference focused on student and faculty rights and responsibilities in general education.

Statewide Collaboration on Outcomes Assessment

The second of our "What Is an Educated Person?" conferences led us to the quagmires of assessment. At that time, Utah's political climate seemed, as in some other states, to ensure the imposition of a particular nationally normed, standardized test. Like other such tests, Utah's proposed test did not overlap with the general education goals the faculty had developed but would be used to evaluate the success of general education. The conference raised so many concerns about the test—and simultaneously issued such a strong statement in favor of alternative forms of assessment—that the regents asked us to help them reconsider the issue. After the third conference, the regents decided to put faculty in charge of assessment. The next year, once assured that results would be issued in a way that did not permit comparisons within or between institutions, faculty developed the tests.

In spring 2001, course-embedded pre- and post-tests were piloted in quantitative literacy, economic history, American history, and American political institutions. The assessment of writing was done through a large-scale writing assessment, using student papers randomly gathered in 2000 and 2001 from English 101 and 201 sections throughout the system. Papers written at the beginning of English 101 counted as pre-tests, and papers written at the end of English 201 counted as post-tests. Analysis of these two sets began in 2002, with teams from all of the state's institutions rating them. Results indicated significant value added from the pre-tests to the post-tests. This approach to writing assessment has been adopted by three of the state's institutions for their own continuing use.

To our knowledge, Utah is the only state that has successfully piloted faculty-led system assessments of general education areas. An assessment of the assessment may therefore be useful for other states. The most thorough analysis is Philip Kramer's dissertation, "Planning, Designing, and Conducting Systemwide Assessment in Higher Education: A Case Study of Utah's General Education Pilot Assessment" (2003). Overall, the positive results of assessment in Utah included statistically significant pre- to post-test improvements in learning. These ranged from 169 percent improvement across pre- to post-test in mathematics, to 36 percent in American history, to 68 percent in economics. Such results should not be a surprise. But they were, even to faculty. After all, if segments of the public were not skeptical of higher education, assessment would not be a public issue.

Other positive results of assessment were found in the attitudes of the faculty who had participated. According to our survey, faculty did not teach to the test, found participating very worthwhile, and were willing to participate again. The regents and the legislature seemed happy as well. In terms of resources, the experiment took huge chunks of faculty time to design, administer, and analyze. But the external test alternatives would have cost much more money. By being embedded in courses, the Utah approach also preserved the student motivation necessary for test results to be meaningful. Because Utah faculty had designed the tests, students participated and their responses were serious—in contrast to student attitudes toward many standardized national tests, including a previous effort in Utah. A final positive outcome was faculty ownership of the curriculum in terms of both the process and the results.

Kramer, whose dissertation analyzed the Utah assessment pilot from a higher education administration point of view, reported additional positive outcomes besides those described above. They included the following:

- Stakeholders, including legislators, clearly agreed that the goal of improving the teaching and learning process was a critically important reason to conduct assessment.
- Many realized that articulating system-wide curricula, courses, degrees, and programs could be conducted in a way that increased curricular coherence, helped faculty become better teachers, and motivated students to become better learners.
- Many came to understand that demonstrating system accountability to internal as well as external stakeholders was an important purpose for conducting the pilot assessment.
- Faculty developed an appreciation for the invaluable role of senior scholars in constructing the assessment tests. Senior scholars facilitated the faculty discussions and the debates on how best to link the pilot assessment to system-wide goals.
- Faculty became more test-savvy. While ultimately they appreciated the strengths of nationally normed instruments, the tests faculty created did reach the basic levels of reliability and validity needed for confidence in the results.

There were negative outcomes too. The huge cost in faculty time was among them. The lack of resources to pay for analysis of qualitative tests except for writing meant that the instruments were multiple-choice questions that did not necessarily tap underlying general education goals. And within jointly developed test banks, individual tests differed because sections themselves differed between instructors and institutions. An additional shortcoming was that the tests measured courses, not full programs of study.

There were quirky disciplinary twists as well. For instance, mathematicians returned the pre-tests, despite possible contamination of the later post-tests, because what counts in mathematics is *how* students arrive at their answers—thus, students needed to see their work. Historians quarreled over which facts were important, so all of the facts wound up in the history test bank. Writing was not strictly "pre" versus "post" at all, except perhaps in some postmodern way. Across fields, test banks included items that from a test-design point of view were clumsy; after all, most faculty are not test-construction experts. Nasty logistical problems of administering the tests' administrators and collecting and coding the data also arose.

Beyond all these specific problems, however, the most important result was positive. The regents, and implicitly the legislature, initially shared some of the national skepticism about the efficacy of general education. That was why they sought assessment. At first, they intended to conduct it annually. But faced with results that demonstrated learning gains, and with evidence that faculty reluctance to assess truly reflects the practical difficulties of the task rather than fear of accountability, the regents suspended the experiment.

Statewide Collaboration on Teaching Evaluations

The task force also explored what we considered a more authentic approach to assessment than the outcomes assessment described above. This approach was based on a model developed by Dair L. Gillespie, an emerita sociologist at the University of Utah. The Gillespie model emphasizes what Shoenberg calls the "intentionality" of general education. Specifically, it asks students to evaluate classes in terms of larger curricular goals discussed at the start of the semester, providing what she argues is an intellectually sounder basis for judging classes than standard instruments. Gillespie proposes that far from systematically answering students' questions about why they have to take certain courses, the usual teaching evaluation instruments suggest contradictory educational purposes and values to students. For instance, the usual instruments ask students to evaluate teachers in terms of enthusiasm and knowledge of subject matter, which implies that good pedagogy means being enthusiastic and that students can competently judge teachers' subject mastery.

The Gillespie teaching evaluation instrument, on the other hand, simply turns course goals into questions, and asks students how the course affected their skills in each area. For instance, if one course goal is to hone critical thinking, then one question on the teaching evaluation instrument asks how much the course improved or diminished the student's ability to think critically. Similarly, if one course goal is quantitative reasoning, then one question taps the effect of the course on that skill. Thus, the very act of completing a teaching evaluation form reminds students (and the faculty they judge) of the course goals. The results provide far more useful feedback to faculty than the admonition to become more "enthusiastic."

Results of piloting the Gillespie approach have been mixed. In Georgia, it did not produce useful information. But at the participating Utah schools, it did. Furthermore, across Utah colleges and classrooms, results varied sufficiently to suggest that the approach taps actual differences in how courses affect general education skills.

Statewide Collaboration with Other Constituencies

Utah's successful emphasis on collaboration and its catholic definition of what constitutes a "general education issue" have promoted conversation about various policy issues related to general education:

- **Advising:** In various focus groups with professional advisers, it has become clear that like the faculty, advisers can become effective proponents for purposeful general education. As with the faculty, the stereotypical adviser who values only courses in the major does not reflect reality—advisers understand and support system-wide general education goals. Now that we know more about this group, advisers have been asked to join the periodic system-wide articulation meetings for the majors as well as for general education, and are invited to the conferences. With system-wide general education goals as a scaffold, Utah also created AdviseUtah, now Utah Mentor, a Web site to promote accurate advising information for parents and students.

- **K–12:** Utah's Student Success initiative, started in 2003, includes K–12 linkages (Utah encourages students to take the first two years of college in high school through advanced placement and dual enrollment, and a special state scholarship rewards those who do). Task force members have been centrally involved in the initiative. A new task force has developed recommendations for improved articulation of the high school curriculum and the general education curriculum. Student Success also involves task force members in conversations with regents, institutional officers, faculty, advisers, and K–12 staff about how to improve high school students' preparation for college general education. To date, only ten states have aligned high school graduation and college English admissions requirements. Only two have done so for math. Utah hopes to be in these vanguards, so task force members helped organize and chair a working conference of high school and college writing and math teachers to improve coordination in these general education areas. Teachers compared their curricula and discussed how to mesh them.

> Collaboration should initially follow the high road, asking "What is an educated person?" rather than dwelling on the mechanics of how to handle the hordes of barbarian transfer students at the gates.

- **Broadening the Faculty Conversation:** At "What Is an Educated Person?" conferences, focus groups periodically revisit the system-wide general education goals that their predecessors developed. These groups include faculty outside as well as inside the particular general education areas under discussion—for instance, engineers participate in the writing group. Conversations with faculty senate members across the state also involve them in the reform effort, as do reports to on-campus curriculum groups. Task force members have joined discussions to promote articulation within the majors, too. And as the three conferences on assessment suggest, a noteworthy quality of new academic values is the very fact of continuing conversations about a topic usually loathed by faculty.

The Moral of the Story

How has all of this happened? In Utah, one of the most important lessons we learned was to enjoy the experience for the political endeavor it is—which means, among other things, knowing and using local contexts. This suggests that what has worked across Utah campuses may prove disastrous elsewhere. Nonetheless, we believe that system-wide general education reform can be built on faculty ownership of the curriculum. Moreover, we believe that if the alternative to collaboration is command, collaboration is preferable. Our experience suggests that collaboration should initially follow the high road, asking "What is an educated person?" rather than dwelling on the mechanics of how to handle the hordes of barbarian transfer students at the gates.

A final lesson from our experience is that the reform process should be made fun. A major reward for activists is the excitement of finally getting to talk with other faculty about intellectual issues—across disciplines at that. We found that this should be encouraged, even if it seemed to take up time that would be better devoted to a forced march through the work at hand. In fact, this *is* part of the work at hand. Fundamentally, system-wide general education reform is not just about the intellectual development of students; it is also about the intellectual nourishment of faculty across the system.

References

Association of American Colleges and Universities. 2002. *Greater expectations: A new vision for learning as a nation goes to college.* Washington, DC: Association of American Colleges and Universities.

Kramer, P. I. 2003. Planning, designing, and conducting systemwide assessment in higher education: A case study of Utah's general education pilot assessment. PhD diss., University of Utah.

Shoenberg, R. 2000. "Why do I have to take this course?" or credit hours, transfer, and curricular coherence. *Peer Review* 2 (2): 4–8.

Providing System Leadership for Student Success
The Case of Georgia

By Dorothy Zinsmeister

How many times have you heard of an adviser or faculty member saying to a student, "Let's get this core course out of the way"? How many times have you heard a faculty member marginalizing the value of courses in the core curriculum? On the other hand, how many times have you spoken with a faculty member who understands the intentions of the core, is able to make connections among courses in the core for students, is familiar with the learning outcomes of courses in the core, and can help students reflect on the value of the core in relationship to the major? These, and other related questions, have been the focus of Georgia's involvement in the Greater Expectations for Student Transfer project.

The Georgia Context: Semester Conversion

In 1995, following many years of debate and discussion, the board of regents ratified the conversion of the University System of Georgia (USG) from quarters to semesters. Over the next two years Georgia redesigned the core curriculum, reconfigured degree programs, and reorganized courses in preparation for the transition to semesters in fall 1997. Semester conversion policies relating to the core curriculum were structured around several guiding principles:

- Each institution's core curriculum follows a common framework and set of principles.
- Standards for student learning are specified.
- An assessment process for general education is mandated.
- The core curriculum completed at one system institution is fully transferable to another system institution.
- A transfer ombudsman at each institution ensures that transferability rules are followed, and that students are not penalized as a result of the conversion to semesters.

Given these guiding principles, Georgia developed a framework for general education that prescribed within disciplinary areas (science, humanities, etc.) common course numbers, titles, and descriptions for virtually all courses in the core curriculum. Each institution had some flexibility in defining its own learning outcomes for the core while at the same time ensuring that the core completed at one institution was transferable to all other institutions within the system.

At the onset of the Greater Expectations for Student Transfer project, Georgia had been using the semester system for just three years. In many ways, the USG was at the right point to benefit from participation in the project, which provided the system with an opportunity to develop common student learning outcomes for the core curriculum, address institutional transfer practices that were occurring outside the system guidelines, and at the same time put in place new guidelines and procedures that had the potential to foster a cohesive learning experience for all students.

> How many times have you spoken with a faculty member who understands the intentions of the core, is familiar with the learning outcomes of courses in the core, and can help students reflect on the value of the core in relationship to the major?

Compared to other state systems of higher education, the University System of Georgia is rather unusual. The system's fifteen two-year colleges, fifteen four-year state universities, and four research universities are governed by an eighteen-member governor-appointed board of regents. The board develops and approves the strategic plan for the system and considers and establishes policy that applies to all thirty-four institutions.

This unique organizational structure and its existing infrastructure support and facilitate much of the work that is undertaken in Georgia. Years ago, and with great foresight, the regents recognized that governing thirty-four institutions with very different missions would require an infrastructure that provided for input and lines of communication among the various institutional sectors. Several structures that supported the Greater Expectations work already existed:

- **Academic Advisory Committees (AACs):** AACs are in place for all of the disciplinary areas that contribute to the core curriculum. Each committee is composed of one faculty representative from each of the thirty-four institutions. The general function of the academic committees is to study the aspects of curricula and programs of instruction within their disciplinary purview and to make recommendations concerning instruction, the exchange of information and ideas, articulation and coordination among the institutions of the university system, and other matters as requested by the chancellor. Although the academic committees make recommendations for core courses in their disciplines, they do not review institutional courses in the disciplines for their sufficiency in meeting the criteria for core courses.

- **Council on General Education**: Created as an extension of the USG Office of the Senior Vice Chancellor for Academics and Fiscal Affairs, the Council on General Education's role is to (a) oversee and maintain the integrity of the USG core curriculum, (b) promote the importance and quality of the core curriculum at the various system institutions, (c) establish criteria that determine which courses are appropriate for inclusion in the core, and (d) ensure the transferability of the core curriculum among the system institutions.

- **Regents' Administrative Committee on Academic Affairs (RACAA):** Composed of the chief academic officers from each of the thirty-four USG institutions, this body meets four times a year to recommend policy to the board of regents, consider recommendations from the academic committees, and discuss other issues forwarded by the chancellor.

Together, the AACs, the council, and RACAA served as crucial avenues for organizing Georgia's work statewide.

Student Transfer Project Strategies

Given the well-developed USG infrastructure, the new framework for the core curriculum, and the system's commitment to core integrity coupled with transferability, the time was right for Georgia to reflect on the intentions and coherence of general education as it related to all students—particularly those who transfer.

The major USG initiatives and activities described below were supported as a result of involvement in the student transfer project. While at first glance they may appear to be unrelated, these activities are actually part of a comprehensive strategy to develop system-wide common student learning outcomes for the core curriculum and common objectives for each course in the core curriculum, to increase awareness of transfer issues, and to provide information to faculty and students that would have a positive impact on students as they move from one institution to another.

Leadership Role of the Council on General Education

Early in the Greater Expectations for Student Transfer project, the Regents' Advisory Committee on Institutional Effectiveness asked the Council on General Education to develop a set of common student learning outcomes for the core curriculum. These outcomes were to be derived from the sets of student learning outcomes submitted by institutions of the university system at the time they undertook conversion from the quarter to the semester calendar. Each institution had some flexibility in defining its own learning outcomes for the core but at the same time had to ensure that the core completed at one institution was transferable to all other system institutions. A comparison of those independently-defined institutional learning outcomes for the core curriculum reveals considerable agreement among all thirty-four institutions. It should not be surprising that Georgia's common framework, principles, and guidelines for the core curriculum resulted in substantial agreement on learning outcomes among all the USG institutions. (The common student learning outcomes for the core curriculum can be found at www.usg.edu/academics/core_curriculum/outcomes.)

From the outset, Georgia recognized that since the student transfer project focused on the intentions of general education within the USG, it made sense to include the Council on General Education as a major partner in the project. In addition to continuing to oversee the core curriculum, the council was charged with promulgating the importance of general education for the system and providing guidelines for the mandated assessment of general education.

This new expanded role for the council led to a recommendation, approved by the chief academic officers in April 2003, that encourages more effective collaboration between two-year and four-year institutions, especially in the core curriculum. Such collaboration requires more effective communication, a greater degree of commitment to the needs of students, and a broader understanding of the natural differences in mission and perspective that exist between two-year and four-year institutions. It also requires a clearly articulated set of expectations within the university system's core curriculum and changes in how the curriculum is embraced at the institutional level.

Transfer Ombudsmen

To help the campus ombudsmen assume their new role as advisers of transfer students, early in fall 2004, the system office personnel and the Council on General Education met with the transfer ombudsmen from each of the thirty-four USG institutions for a workshop that offered an overview of the core curriculum principles and framework, reviewed transfer policies and procedures, and discussed the responsibilities of the transfer ombudsman position. The workshop also included discussion of actual case studies and covered the Curriculum, Advising, and Program Planning tool (CAPP), which assists students, faculty, and administrators with core curriculum, advising, and transfer issues.

Mini-Core Project

Georgia has two state-supported systems of higher education, the University System of Georgia (USG) and the Department of Technical and Adult Education (DTAE). USG institutions contribute to the educational, cultural, economic, and social advancement of Georgia by providing undergraduate general education and programs leading to associate, baccalaureate, master's, professional, and doctoral degrees. Its mission includes pursuing leading-edge basic and applied research, scholarly inquiry, and creative endeavors. DTAE, on the other hand, is a system of thirty-four institutions that provides technical education, customized business and industry training, and adult education in Georgia. Students transfer between the two systems, and individual USG institutions have articulation agreements with individual DTAE institutions.

What distinguishes the "mini-core project" from most other articulation agreements is that it represents a collaborative agreement between two separate postsecondary education systems. Supported by the governor, the commissioner of DTAE, and the chancellor of the USG, the "mini-core project" resulted in an agreement between USG institutions and DTAE institutions to transfer degree-required basic skills courses in English and mathematics. Drawing on the expertise of the AACs in English and mathematics, faculty from both systems met in workshops over an eighteen-month period to work toward consensus on common content standards and admission, placement, and exit criteria for the "mini-core" courses. English and mathematics faculty members from the institutions reviewed the standards and outcomes for their respective courses and signed off on them—albeit reluctantly in some cases.

The English and the mathematics faculties from the two systems now have a much better understanding of what each is trying to accomplish in these basic skills courses. Because course criteria and competencies were developed and widely shared, full-time, part-time, and temporary faculty now have a road map to follow when preparing students to succeed regardless of where they complete their degree programs.

Those who interact often with faculty know that work like this is difficult among faculty *within* a university system; it is still more difficult among faculty *between* two systems. Even after misconceptions about each of the systems are addressed, new understandings often go unheeded or are forgotten. As the work proceeds, keeping accurate records of decisions made and the rationale for making them is paramount.

Faculty Surveys

In spring 2001, twenty-three USG institutions agreed to participate in a faculty survey to gather baseline data on awareness of the statewide general education initiative, perceptions of the relative importance of general education, awareness of learning goals in general education courses, and attitudes about the value of assessment. Targeted in the survey were full-time and part-time biology, English, and mathematics faculty teaching courses in the core curriculum.

Like Maryland, Georgia made the assumption that the survey's findings would have general applicability to most other disciplines. In addition to providing baseline data as a launching point for future activities, the survey raised awareness about general education and transfer perceptions, and data from the survey prompted institutional discussions by discipline on learning outcomes for courses in the core curriculum among faculty members in the state. One of the more interesting—and perhaps also disturbing—findings was that 78 percent of faculty who teach in courses in the core curriculum believe that shared acceptance, communication, and assessment of learning outcomes is positive at their own institutions, but only 34 percent believe that these learning outcomes are shared by instructors at the other institutions in the system. There is also a wide disparity in the level of satisfaction with the assessment of learning outcomes in general education among faculty who teach general education courses (83 percent satisfied), faculty in the same department who do not teach general education courses (60 percent), and faculty on other USG campuses who do not teach general education courses (24 percent). So although the USG touts a system-wide transfer policy that allows students to transfer general education coursework among institutions, the quality and assessment of that coursework is suspect—even among faculty in the same department.

Focus Groups

Data from the faculty surveys informed a series of focus groups that allowed us to expand on the survey questions and to gather general education perceptions from groups on campus other than faculty members. An external consultant led three focus groups: one consisting of administrators who coordinate general education at their institutions; one made up of administrators involved in student advisement; and a third made up of teaching faculty. The information collected during the focus groups was consistent with that obtained from the faculty surveys, but also provided some suggestions for change to share with the transfer ombudsmen on each campus. For example, focus group participants proposed methods to increase faculty support for and involvement in the general education program, and ideas for either change or improvement of current practices. In particular, the focus group summaries and faculty survey data have guided the academic committees, our work with the transfer ombudsmen, and the proactive stance of the Council on General Education.

Charge to Academic Committees

Results from the faculty surveys pointed to the need to raise the awareness of the general education learning goals and to clarify how the goals for individual courses in the core curriculum contributed to general outcomes. The vehicles chosen to begin this work were the Academic Advisory Committees. Each committee was charged with reviewing each course and preparing a set of learning outcomes common to all the institutions. Fourteen committees have been discussing, arguing, and articulating the learning outcomes for core courses. Many of the learning outcomes are completed and posted on the USG core curriculum Web site (www.usg.edu/academics/comm). We believe that showcasing the learning outcomes will suggest connections between and among core courses. We also believe that they will inform faculty and student advisers about the intentions of the course, and help answer the question "Why do I have to take this course?"

Not surprisingly, however, individual departments represented by the AACs do not want to relinquish the little (perceived) autonomy they have, and believe that they deserve more. Conversations in the AACs swirled around issues related to academic freedom or academic standards and assessment, often involving profound misconceptions about the meaning and application of those concepts. The word "standard," for example, was often misinterpreted as referring to "standardizing" the curriculum. The need to develop system-wide learning outcomes for courses in the core—making intentions of the courses clear to faculty and to students—frequently reminded the AACs of the importance of completing the task.

Annual USG Teaching and Learning Conferences

Findings from our faculty surveys and focus groups led us to develop agendas for annual statewide Teaching and Learning conferences designed to stimulate discussion on the purposes of general education and to provide some very practical strategies for assessment of general education goals. Attendance at the conference, which consisted of teams of four or five faculty leaders from each campus, was predicated on the understanding that each team would develop and implement a teaching and learning project upon returning to the campus. Some examples of proposed projects include "Back to Basics: How to Develop Assessable Goals and Objectives," "Assessment of Competencies in the General Education Core," "Keys to a Successful Freshman Experience," and "Showcasing Assessment of Student Critical Thinking." Conference participants expressed a real interest in the conference topics. Designing ways to continue the dialogue once participants return to campus is the challenge.

Curriculum, Advising, and Program Planning (CAPP)

As the USG was moving forward with its student transfer project activities, it was engaged in other initiatives that fostered and supported student transfer. One of these, CAPP, is a flexible degree audit tool that allows students to track progress toward their educational goals. Its purpose is to improve advisement, provide students with access to their degree information, improve distribution of information to students and faculty, and facilitate articulation among USG institutions. One major component of CAPP is the identification of course and program attributes to allow for standardization across the system. What this means for an institution is a course-for-course transfer articulation with the other USG institutions. Making learning outcomes clear across the system for courses in the core becomes especially important as more and more institutions implement CAPP.

> The long-term goal must be to ensure that we are assessing twenty-first-century outcomes for twenty-first-century students.

Summer Meeting of Academic and Student Affairs

Each summer, the Regents' Administrative Committees on Academic Affairs and on Student Affairs meet jointly to focus on a theme for the coming year. The Association of American Colleges and Universities' *Greater Expectations* report (2002) was chosen as the focus for the 2004–5 discussions.

Conclusion

Prior to Georgia's participation in the Greater Expectations for Student Transfer project, students enrolled in institutions in the University System of Georgia enjoyed guaranteed transferability of the core curriculum and a guaranteed commitment to core curriculum and general education learning outcomes. Course numbers, course titles, and course descriptions for most core curriculum courses are the same across the system, yet faculty have not been confident that system disciplinary colleagues or even departmental colleagues meet the same high standards for rigorous course content and course learning outcomes.

Greater Expectations for Student Transfer in Georgia was a three-year odyssey that aimed to strengthen the role of the Council on General Education in educating faculty and students about the goals and intentions of general education and in making course learning objectives transparent to both faculty and students. We addressed these goals through a variety of strategies, and in some cases made significant progress. The council has crafted a formal statement of the purposes of the USG's statewide general education requirements that is ready for system-wide distribution, enlisted the cooperation of the transfer ombudsmen to serve as "disciples" of general education on each of the campuses, and supported electronic advising and planning structures that inform students of the purposes of general education. We have effectively moved from providing leadership from the system office to providing direction and support to the institutions. What will follow next year are efforts to lead the system to purposeful assessment of student learning, efforts that we hope will lead to purposeful learning experiences across all institutions. We are not done yet. The long-term goal must be to ensure that we are assessing twenty-first-century outcomes for twenty-first-century students.

Reference

Association of American Colleges and Universities. 2002. *Greater expectations: A new vision for learning as a nation goes to college.* Washington, DC: Association of American Colleges and Universities.

Building Statewide Partnerships for Student Success
The Case of Maryland

By Nancy S. Shapiro, Teri Hollander, and Jennifer Vest Frank

Maryland higher education policy exists within a very particular K–16 context that has become increasingly important over the past ten years. The state's K–16 initiative, which reflects its commitment to creating a seamless educational experience for students from kindergarten through college, was launched in 1995. At that time, the chancellor of the University System of Maryland (USM) joined forces with the state superintendent of schools and the higher education secretary to raise student achievement, improve college readiness, and address issues around access and success for poor and minority students.

Working with a seed grant from the Pew Charitable Trusts, the three cochairs of the newly formed K–16 partnership announced plans to establish a community of teachers, faculty, administrators, and business partners who would form a leadership team to address the challenges of preparing all students to graduate from college. The first generation of work on this project focused on establishing clear high school graduation requirements that would guarantee that all students were ready for college or a career upon graduation. That work, which included standards setting and development of high school assessments, led to a major education reform initiative in the state, also supported and promoted by the K–16 coalition. Since 2000, with initiatives such as the federal No Child Left Behind Act and the new Teacher Quality Standards, the value and virtue of the K–16 coalition has become even more important.

The Maryland Context

All components of Maryland's higher education system make substantial contributions to educational access in the state. Nearly half of Maryland's public high school graduates progress to an in-state two- or four-year institution. About a quarter of the students enrolled in the two-year institutions transfer to a four-year institution, adding significantly to the number of first-time entrants to the state's four-year colleges and universities. The magnitude of student transfer and the expected growth in transfer entrants highlight the need for careful cooperation among two-year and four-year colleges in transfer admissions and in developing coherent general education programs.

The Greater Expectations for Student Transfer project is thus embedded in the K–16 context, and we have found that the K–16 structures put in place for other purposes (such as alignment and teacher education) can also serve the purposes of the transfer project. Working to define outcomes in the high school arena carries over to the work that must be done to define outcomes in college curricula, especially as we attempt to generalize those outcomes across segments (two-year and four-year, public and private).

From the outset of Maryland's K–16 work, the state realized that it had to help faculty and teachers understand what it means to develop an outcomes-based curriculum and accountability system. Definition of learning outcomes—what students must know and be able to do—is a major part of the work of K–16 and the student transfer project. Maryland has been engaged in defining common learning outcomes for several years and through those efforts has learned a great deal about how to structure an alignment process for success. The Association of American Colleges and Universities (AAC&U) transfer project enabled Maryland to push forward with this work and disseminate the work more broadly across the state.

The Development of Outcomes-Based General Education Requirements

When AAC&U invited Maryland to join in its Greater Expectations for Student Transfer project, Maryland already had a strong record of K–16 collaboration across segments that served as a platform for the next level of development of general education outcomes. Over the six years of the project, Maryland made significant progress toward reaching the state goals. General education and transfer articulation are particularly important in Maryland since community colleges currently enroll almost half of all undergraduate students in the state. More than half of all students who transfer into one of the state's four-year public institutions and more than half of those who graduate from Maryland's public four-year colleges got their start at a Maryland community college.

The Board of Regents of the University System of Maryland governs all but two of the public four-year colleges and universities in the state. Although there is a great deal of collaboration between two- and four-year colleges, the two-year community colleges are not included in the university system. Transfer and articulation issues are addressed through collaboration and intersegmental negotiation, in conjunction with the Maryland Higher Education Commission.

In 1993, USM institutions were close to capacity enrollment, and thus community college enrollments rose. As the community college transfer population grew, the higher education community looked for a streamlined way to address the particular needs of transfer students while maintaining high standards for undergraduate education outcomes. The vice chancellor for academic affairs convened a group of two-year and four-year chief academic officers and charged them with facilitating articulation and transfer. This group was designated the Intersegmental Chief Academic Officers (ICAO) Group, and eventually assumed responsibility for the broad umbrella discussions of general education requirements.

The ICAOs identified the transfer of general education requirements as one of the most pressing issues facing Maryland higher education. They agreed to create an ongoing forum to address the ways in which a coherent program of study could be aligned between the two segments. In the interim, the Maryland Higher Education Commission proposed new general education regulations that would establish a "one-size-fits-all" core for both two-year and four-year public institutions. A prescribed program of forty-five credits would be imposed, leaving the two-year institutions with little room to integrate major requirements, and no room for any institution to develop a coherent and meaningful general education program that was intentionally designed to meet the individual goals of the institution.

This unilateral action on the part of the Maryland Higher Education Commission motivated the ICAOs to accelerate their deliberations regarding general education. In December 1993, the group proposed an alternative course of action: rather than transfer course by course, the ICAOs suggested program transfers designed around learning outcomes. The Maryland Higher Education Commission accepted the alternative and promulgated the new general education and transfer regulations in fall 1994.

Although the commission was pleased with the result, the chief academic officers' group felt that the real work had just begun. They began to struggle with how best to implement the new regulations while providing enough curricular autonomy for institutions to make the general education requirements a coherent, intentional, and integrated part of the degree. With this commitment, the ICAOs convened themselves as a standing body, and developed a set of guiding principles for general education that continue to be enhanced, revised, and discussed.

Faculty discipline groups are the formal structures through which the articulation of general education courses (including standards, goals, and learning outcomes) occurs in Maryland. Over the course of AAC&U's student transfer project, faculty discipline groups were convened and supported in the physical sciences, biological sciences, English literature, mathematics, and the fine and performing arts. These faculty discipline groups developed definitional criteria, course competencies, and student outcomes for general education courses to correspond with the 1996 requirements of the Maryland Higher Education Commission and the 1997 recommendations of the Maryland Intersegmental Chief Academic Officers Group.

The participation of faculty, which was essential to the success of the project, was dependent on the support and priority given to this work by the chief academic officers. A total of 106 faculty members from the five discipline areas were nominated for participation by their campus provosts or chief academic officers, representing a total of twelve two-year institutions and twelve four-year institutions. (The charge to the committees, draft outcomes, and reports are available online at mdcao.usmd.edu/comm.html.)

Rather than developing a standard statewide curriculum for general education or a common course numbering system in the Maryland Code of Regulations, two-year and four-year institutions committed themselves to developing common sets of standards, goals, and learning outcomes in each general education discipline area. Thus, the role of faculty became central in facilitating the effective articulation of general education courses across the state and in ensuring that students would have a cohesive learning experience, determined by the shared definition of learning outcomes among the institutions of higher education, as they moved from institution to institution.

The Student Transfer Project in Maryland

The key to the success of Maryland's approach to the Greater Expectations for Student Transfer project was the involvement of two-year and four-year faculty in every stage of the process. The Maryland project drew on faculty who served as teachers of general education, as advisers of transfer students, and as facilitators of the articulation of general education courses across institutions. In order to increase faculty awareness of general education and transfer issues, encourage them to share information and experiences, and provide them with resources and support, we planned a variety of activities and strategies. While many of these activities were coordinated centrally through the University System of Maryland, others were initiated by individual colleges and universities, regional consortia of two-year and four-year institutions, or discipline-based alliances across institutions. USM has a tradition of bringing together diverse segments, finding funding sources, and then distributing funds in ways that enable multiple partners to participate and give legitimacy to statewide academic collaborations.

Between 2001 and 2003, the Greater Expectations for Student Transfer project supported a number of major activities that pushed the transfer alignment issues forward. The brief descriptions below suggest the types of initiatives that are necessary to build a coherent statewide understanding of general education outcomes.

Statewide General Education Faculty Survey

Recognizing the need to establish a "beginning" for this project, in April 2001 USM administered a thirty-item survey through the campus chief academic officers to gather baseline data about faculty attitudes, expectations, and experiences related to general education and transfer articulation both at individual institutions and across Maryland. We targeted two-year and four-year faculty in biology, English, and mathematics to parallel the survey that was being conducted in Georgia and Utah for this project, but we were also aware that the findings would have general applicability to most other disciplines. While it is true that graduate students and part-time lecturers teach many sections of general education courses at research universities, the majority of survey responses were from full-time faculty. We received a total of 641 usable faculty responses from twenty-three two- and four-year institutions in Maryland. In addition to providing informative baseline data as a launching point for discussion, the survey also raised awareness about general education and transfer articulation among faculty across the state.

Through the survey, the university system found that

- only 23 percent of responding faculty were aware of state-level initiatives aimed at easing student transfer among public colleges and universities in Maryland;
- only 20 percent of responding faculty were aware of state-level initiatives aimed at developing more intellectual coherence among general education courses at public colleges and universities in Maryland;
- only 6 percent of responding faculty were aware of the general education work of the ICAOs, and only 8 percent were aware of the work of the general education faculty discipline groups;
- 68 percent of the responding faculty considered the transfer of general education courses very important.

The survey also asked faculty to provide an informal assessment of the entering students' levels of preparation for their college courses. We asked this question because, in some circles, general education requirements are seen as a barrier to graduation. To those audiences, in particular, it is important to communicate not only the purposes of general education, but also why students may have difficulty completing the general education curriculum successfully. When asked to rate levels of student preparation for meeting the learning goals in their general education courses, 31 percent of the faculty reported that students tended to be not at all prepared or poorly prepared, 52 percent reported that they were somewhat prepared, and 17 percent reported that they were prepared or very well prepared. While 93 percent of the responding faculty thought that the learning goals in their general education courses were likely shared by other faculty teaching the same course in their department, only 32 percent thought that these goals were likely shared by faculty teaching the same course at other colleges and universities.

These statistics suggest that although faculty intellectually agree that general education outcomes are an important part of a college education, they are unaware of the extent of the effort in the state to develop common learning outcomes, and they are even less confident that their colleagues across the state in other institutions share their "standards" for determining successful achievement of the standards.

Statewide General Education Conference

Armed with these findings, we prepared our work in the state by organizing a statewide general education conference in November 2001. This conference was designed to raise awareness of state-level general education and transfer initiatives, to provide information and resources for faculty who teach general education courses, and to facilitate communication and collaboration related to general education and articulation across different institutions and educational segments.

The success of this conference can be best measured by the subsequent activities that grew out of the conversations that took place over those two days. The conference was designed to initiate a statewide discussion of general education. The working groups that formed during the conference were given an opportunity to apply for mini-grants from AAC&U's student transfer project that would enable them to continue their work throughout the next two years. The direct outcome of this conference was the "seeding" of several such mini-projects.

DACUM Conference on Communication Competencies in the General Education Curriculum

The first of these follow-up activities was organized by communications faculty at Prince George's Community College and the University of Maryland, College Park. The primary goal of the Developing a Curriculum (DACUM) conference was to certify the validity of the oral communication competencies that were approved by the Maryland Communication Association in 1989 and the Maryland Intersegmental Chief Academic Officers Group in 1999. DACUM is an organizational process for collecting all the relevant perceptions and facts about a topic, and refining them, consolidating them, testing them, and endorsing the results as common or shared understandings. Recommendations from the conference were used to refine the competencies, make necessary revisions, and provide clarifications to the speech and communication component of general education.

Western Maryland General Education Conference

A second outcome of the statewide conference was a regional conference planned by western Maryland institutions. This regional meeting sought to engage faculty in examining the interrelationships among institutional goals for general education, the twenty-first-century expectations as outlined at the statewide general education conference, and the Middle States requirements for the assessment of general education. The meeting offered faculty an opportunity to examine the implications of the *Greater Expectations* report (AAC&U 2002) within their disciplines and discuss ideas for cross-campus collaboration.

Participants at the regional conference expressed an eagerness to continue the dialogue—suggesting that much of the value of such meetings is that they serve as the starting point, not the ending point, for alignment work. For any reliable, coherent work on general education curriculum alignment to occur, USM has found, such face-to-face meetings must take place.

Mathematics Placement Testing and Bridge Goals Conference

A third outgrowth of the statewide conference was the furthering of the complex general education mathematics agenda. Mathematicians have built a strong statewide community in Maryland, in part because so much depends on clearly articulated expectations for student success in the field. From prior research on K–16 issues, USM knew that mathematics posed a significant hurdle to many postsecondary students. Over 30 percent of students at Maryland colleges and universities are placed in remedial mathematics courses, and national data show that students who have more than one remedial semester frequently fail to complete a degree at all.

With these specific challenges in mind, participants at the mathematics meeting spent the day addressing student placement testing. In May 2003, under the auspices of the transfer project, Howard Community College sponsored a statewide conference to provide mathematics faculty with the opportunity to learn about "item response theory" in the context of student placement testing and to discuss the appropriate placement test cutoff scores for entering college students in Maryland.

In May 2004, the mathematics group presented final recommendations for what they call the "Mathematics Bridge Goals": a set of clear expectations for bridging the gap between high school exit standards and college readiness standards. These recommendations have the potential to create a breakthrough that may even lead to a common placement examination, aligned with high school exit exams, for both community colleges and four-year colleges. It has always been clear to mathematicians that the value of mathematics in general education lies in the analytical reasoning that it requires, and now USM has a framework for building a message that goes beyond the mathematics community.

In the past, K–12 mathematics faculty members have chided higher education for setting them up for failure. In their struggle to align mathematics curricula with multiple placement assessments and multiple entry-level expectations, high school mathematics teachers felt like they were shooting at a moving target. By developing the definitions of outcomes for general education mathematics, the mathematics committee has enabled the high school mathematics community to move forward with high school assessments that will be meaningful for all members of the K–16 partnership.

Statewide English Composition Conferences
Every year since the state conference on general education, the transfer project has supported a K–16 English composition conference, inviting faculty from two- and four-year colleges to come together to discuss student writing samples and bring examples of promising teaching practices. In the spirit of spreading the message about expectations for college, high school English teachers are also invited to participate in the conferences. Given such problems as paying for substitutes for high school teachers, it is difficult to get the secondary school instructors in the same room with college faculty members.

> We discovered that the dialogue across K–16 expanded our understanding exponentially.

Yet we discovered that the dialogue across K–16 expanded our understanding exponentially. As a result of these conferences, our community has developed deeper comprehension of the cultural constraints that govern each segment of composition and English faculties.

Intersegmental Secondary AAT Faculty Discipline Groups
Over the past three years, parallel to the work on general education and transfer, Maryland has been struggling to respond to statewide teacher shortages in mathematics, chemistry, physics, and Spanish. In fall 2003, the K–16 Leadership Council asked a group of higher education faculty and administrators to develop a working model of defined articulation that would build seamless transfer pathways into the teacher education programs across the state, both public and private. This work led to the development of a new degree in Maryland in 2004, the associate of arts of teaching (AAT).

The process of developing this degree forced Maryland to address problems that cut across all states trying to do alignment work: inconsistent standards, misaligned programs, and the frustrations inherent in complex systems of independent agencies.

While the AAT is specifically designed to build a pipeline for future teachers, in developing the degree the state engaged in a massive articulation enterprise that has profound implications for transfer. Groups of faculty in each of the shortage areas were charged with developing a common set of learning outcomes for the first two years of the disciplinary major that will articulate with the remaining two years of the major at all public and independent four-year institutions in the state (for examples of these outcomes, see mdk16.usmd.edu/inside.php?area_id=69). Each group consisted of two-year, four-year, and K–12 faculty members. The yearlong exercise brought into sharp relief all prior discussions of learning outcomes. We found that for the first several months of this process, faculty in the various disciplinary groups needed background in defining, framing, and assessing learning outcomes. Once we crossed that threshold with the faculty groups, the process of reaching agreement among two-year and four-year faculty was remarkably smooth. Agreement on these outcomes will ensure that all students who begin their education at a public two-year college in Maryland will be able to smoothly transfer to a four-year public or private college in Maryland without losing any credits.

Conclusion

It is our hope and our expectation that we have accomplished three things that will change the way general education is delivered in Maryland. First, many more faculty members are more keenly aware that general education is a responsibility of the entire higher education community. It is not limited to a single campus "self study" or accreditation report; rather, the discussion must cross campuses, institutions, and segments. To paraphrase John Donne: "No campus is an island." Second, statewide programs that have been developed based on outcomes defined by faculties from both two-year and four-year colleges have generated strong connections between segments that will benefit students. Finally, some—though not enough—high school teachers have been brought into the dialogue about the outcomes of general education, and some—not enough—college faculty members have been brought into the conversation about high school standards and learning outcomes. As a result, some students—though still not enough—will have the benefit of a seamless transition that is the goal of a K–16 framework for education.

Reference

Association of American Colleges and Universities. 2002. *Greater expectations: A new vision for learning as a nation goes to college.* Washington, DC: Association of American Colleges and Universities.

Intentionality and Coherence in Undergraduate General Education
What Have We Learned?

By Martin Finkelstein

The Association of American Colleges and Universities (AAC&U) has conducted a very ambitious project that addresses significant challenges to providing all college students with a demanding and relevant general education. Greater Expectations for Student Transfer took as its point of departure two central sets of questions:

1. To what extent are students and teachers, on the inside, and public officials and trustees, on the outside, aware of and clear about the purposes of general education in today's society? And to what extent are those purposes reflected in courses labeled as "general education" as they are currently offered? What interventions can policy makers and educational leaders undertake to enhance awareness and clarity of purpose of general education courses?

2. In the new era of massive state systems, the majority of students now enroll at two or more colleges (both two-year and four-year) before receiving their baccalaureate degrees. The majority no longer complete their general education programs at a single institution. Under these circumstances, to what extent is there sufficient *sharing* of intentions across campuses to allow for a coherent student experience at multiple institutions in a single state system? Who is responsible for assuring such coherence and what are appropriate strategies for doing so?

Through the course of this project, the assumption that the answers to most of these questions are negative has been confirmed. It is clear that institutions are operating in the absence of both clarity and coherence of purpose, and that state systems have a key role to play in ensuring both. General education has, in short, become an important state policy issue.

Three Different Systems

Greater Expectations for Student Transfer brought together educational leaders from three very different states. Through the project, these leaders learned from one another and advanced the goals of intentionality and coherence in general education.

In Georgia, where a centralized board of regents oversees the entire public sector (except, until 2003, the technical institutes), it was the regents who took the lead. While making the transition from a quarter to a semester system between 1995 and 1997, Georgia's regents adopted a common course numbering system across the state's thirty-four campuses and defined the scope and content of the state system's general education requirement. To support implementation of these policies, the regents created two key infrastructural elements: the Council on General Education (charged with approval of all courses to bear the "general education" designation) and nearly three dozen system-wide disciplinary committees composed of faculty (typically department chairs) with campus leadership roles in undergraduate education.

At the other extreme, Utah adopted a highly participatory, faculty-driven approach to ensuring the intentionality and coherence of general education courses. An ad hoc statewide task force composed primarily of faculty convened a series of public conversations about the meaning of general education that was open to faculty, administrators, legislators, and the media. Early in its existence, in response to legislative concern about accountability, this task force persuaded the regents to allow faculty to develop a pilot assessment program in three required areas of study: writing, mathematics, and American institutions.

In Maryland, activities were shaped by a very active K–16 reform initiative organized around two efforts. First, to promote discussion of general education outcomes and to define outcomes in particular curricular areas, Maryland established a statewide associate of arts in teaching program that required the general education programs of two-year colleges to articulate seamlessly with teacher education programs at the eleven University of Maryland system campuses. Second, the state defined what high school graduates need to know in order to be fully prepared for (and succeed in) the first year of college. This effort forced college faculty across the state to work together to clarify their expectations of what high school graduates should know when they enter college.

This chapter reflects on the major evaluation challenges faced by these three states. It describes responses to those challenges, details the project's accomplishments (intended and unintended), and offers some conclusions about project evaluation and about statewide initiatives to improve general education.

The project evaluation, while intimately related to the "stories" of the individual states, also had a story of its own—a story of ambitious plans and assumptions stubbornly held and reluctantly abandoned. It begins with a description of how the project evaluation was conceptualized and designed, how ambitions and assumptions were tempered by early results, and how those results shaped subsequent work. It concludes with a few of the "big" lessons learned—about the functions and roles of evaluation as well as about the vicissitudes of general education as a public policy issue.

The Initial Challenge

One of the first critical tasks of the student transfer project was to articulate an overarching set of national goals that were related to the agendas of the individual states but sufficiently distinguishable to constitute a coherent, project-specific agenda. Once these goals were identified, the project needed to secure the commitment of participants and to coordinate the national goals with the individualized agendas of the three participating states. The table below shows how the project's goals were represented by the end of the first year.

Table 1. A Schematic Representation of the Greater Expectations for Student Transfer Project

Goals	Activities	Outcomes	Indicators	Means of Assessment
Clarify intentions of statewide general education requirements	Discussions among cognizant groups at state level	Formal statements of intention	The statements	
Make these intentions clear to faculty	Statewide conferences; conversations on individual campuses; propagation of formal statements of intention	Better answers to the question, "Why do I have to take this course?"; general education courses taught to the purposes of the requirements	Improved faculty understanding of general education purposes; syllabi that reflect these purposes	Faculty survey; syllabus analysis; focus groups
Make these intentions clear to nonfaculty advisers	Joint faculty/ nonfaculty conversations (Utah)	Improved ability to articulate general education purposes		Focus groups
Make these intentions clear to students	Develop improved written materials; put information about intentions on advising Web site (Georgia, Utah)	Improved student understanding of general education purposes	New advising materials; outcomes assessment (Utah); student perception that general education goals are being addressed in courses	Standardized surveys of student satisfaction; "Gillespie questions"; focus groups

In an effort to leaven state assessment efforts with a continuous infusion of national perspective (and vice versa), local evaluation teams that included the project evaluator, the state coordinator for the project, and a doctoral student in higher education administration from a local research university were organized. While the project evaluator met annually with the doctoral students from all three states as a national evaluation team, the doctoral students were encouraged to work closely with their state coordinators, who provided an independent source of evaluation support on the ground.

Next Steps: Designing the Means

After defining a set of national project outcomes, the next logical step was to develop a set of indicators across the three states that would at once provide a baseline snapshot of the project's point of departure and the benchmarks against which to document changes over the course of the project. As the project evaluator, I collaborated with the state coordinators and the project director on identifying potential quantitative, operational indicators. While guided by the ambitious premise that our job was to design an information infrastructure capable of monitoring state progress in the achievement of general education goals, we recognized the need to be as unobtrusive as possible. To that end, we identified at least three existing data streams in the three states:

1. **Statewide Student Surveys:** Both Utah and Georgia had recently contracted with ACT to periodically administer the Student Opinion Survey (SOS). The SOS includes several questions about students' satisfaction with their educational experience, and responses to these questions can be compared across transfer and non-transfer student subgroups, across sectors and across majors, etc. Maryland has encouraged its public campuses to administer periodically the College Student Experience Questionnaire, the data collection instrument used by the National Survey of Student Engagement to monitor the intensity of student involvement with various aspects of their college experience.

2. **Student Course Evaluations:** In Utah, several faculty members had periodically added a question to the end-of-semester student course evaluation forms for selected general education courses at Utah State and the University of Utah. The question specifically asked students to what extent the course affected their skills or competencies in general education areas such as analyzing and critically evaluating information resources, developing aesthetic appreciation, and appreciating human diversity. Chief academic officers in Georgia and Maryland were asked to consider adding such a question to their standard student course evaluation forms for at least some courses meeting the general education requirements.

3. **Actual Course Syllabi:** We collected syllabi for general education courses in biology, English, and mathematics and planned to compare them to syllabi two years later with the

following questions in mind: To what extent, and in what ways, have the statements of course goals and objectives changed in the direction of greater convergence with state outcomes and goals? To what extent, and in what ways, have assignments changed to reflect the state goals and outcomes for general education? To what extent, and in what ways, has assessment of students in the general education courses changed to more precisely mirror state outcomes and goals?

To these existing streams, we added two more:

4. **Faculty Awareness and Attitudes:** Since it is the faculty members who deliver general education to students, faculty must be both aware of statewide general education goals and intended outcomes and able to communicate them to their students. In order to assess faculty awareness and communication to students, Georgia and Maryland conducted a survey of instructors in the key general education courses of English composition, mathematics, and biology.

5. **Other Stakeholder Perceptions:** Data from three additional sources were readily collectible and potentially useful for assessing the achievement of project goals. These included "official" statements by state governments about the nature and purposes of general education as contained in official documents and in several project-sponsored forums for state higher education executive officers; data from campus transfer advisers and general education program administrators, including results from several focus groups made up of student advisers; and student data, including the results of focus groups on student general education experience as well more unobtrusive indicators of students' information-seeking behavior (such as the number of hits on student advising Web sites).

First Fruits? A Test of Our Basic Premises

The faculty survey produced some dramatic, if not surprising, results in Georgia and Maryland. The survey showed that the majority of faculty statewide (other than the small minority who actually were direct participants in initiatives in their respective states) were relatively unaware of state initiatives to address coherence and intentionality in general education programs. However, the majority of faculty felt that intentionality and coherence of general education coursework were important, if not urgent, issues for policy *in departments and at campuses other than their own.* In other words, they saw themselves as communicating clearly to students the goals of general education, but they were not so sure about others.

These findings clarified the magnitude of the "awareness" gap between the teaching faculty on the ground and statewide general education faculty leaders (typically department chairs) with regard to the state's general education goals and agenda. The findings also suggested that while there was a dim perception of a general education problem, it was perceived primarily as a problem for other campuses. Given the stark differences between the relatively small number of state project participants and the number of rank-and-file faculty, these early results focused our collective attention on faculty infrastructure issues. Project leaders needed to identify the mechanisms that already existed or might be put in place to extend dialogue effectively from the statewide level to individual campuses, individual departments, and even individual faculty members, so that they might take ownership of the problem.

Each statewide project addressed these infrastructure and ownership issues in different ways. In Georgia and Maryland, standing cross-campus disciplinary committees were established to shape and monitor general education in the disciplines. In Utah, statewide and regional dialogues were convened to address the question, "What is an educated person?"

Early quantitative research also raised more general and disturbing questions about the basic premises undergirding our evaluation plan. The evaluation team had assumed first that our project evaluation should focus on the development of an information infrastructure within the states capable of monitoring faculty attitudes and practices, student understanding of the intentions of their general education courses, and the efficiency of transfer across public institutions and sectors. In short, we sought to build the capacity of state systems to monitor their policy objectives for general education over the long term. This goal was based on several assumptions, some of which turned out to be quite tenuous:

- that it is possible to sustain commitment to long-term information capacity building goals among state coordinators and staff when the payoff is neither clear nor immediate
- that it is easier to "piggyback" on existing information systems and their protocols and thus avoid burdening state project coordinators with a new set of housekeeping tasks than it is to conduct ad hoc data collection efforts specific to certain constituencies and certain project goals at relevant times
- that data are perceived primarily—or even partly—in terms of their benign descriptive value for assessing achievement of policy goals, and not in terms of their less than benign political valence

Our initial results challenged the notion that for this project the primary utility of generating baseline data was to create the benchmark for future data collection rather than an immediate guide for action in navigating current policy debates. It was, in short, extremely difficult to sustain the commitment to the development of a research effort and infrastructure over the long term. Instead, project leaders seized upon the obvious immediate uses of the data as one-time fodder for faculty and staff development. Thus, in both Georgia and Maryland, ambitious plans for repeating faculty and student surveys had the wind knocked rather quickly from their collective sails, and equally ambitious plans for introducing new data collection instruments, or even adaptations of existing instruments (e.g. student course evaluations), quickly flagged in the face of local campus inertia, resistance to administrative meddling with faculty evaluation instruments, and a lack of local project staff and resources to complete the associated research tasks.

Thus the initial intent to establish baseline indicators and create a data infrastructure for monitoring general education practices and outcomes metamorphosed into an effort to use information for its immediate payoff and to gain insight into the process whereby general education was moved onto the public policy agenda. Other key concerns included how general education was linked to other statewide agenda items, and how each state's initiatives were sustained over time. To that end, each state agreed to prepare a case study that focused on a common "checklist" of basic information as an integral piece in the project evaluation plan.

Lessons Learned

The lessons learned from the evaluation are organized roughly around four themes:

1. getting general education on the public policy agenda
2. moving policy concerns from the state level to action on the ground at the campus and even the individual department level
3. understanding the political life of information, or how information capability is developed while managing its political valence
4. sustaining reform over time when no new resources are forthcoming

Getting General Education on the State Policy Agenda

In none of the three states did qualitative concerns about the intentions and coherence of general education find their way directly onto the public policy agenda. For the most part, they "piggybacked" on other issues. The issue of transfering credit from one public institution, typically a two-year institution, to another institution, typically a four-year institution, was most commonly used to guide public discussion. Indeed, in many states, difficulties in transferring credit among public institutions has generated a good deal of concern among the basic constituencies of legislators as frustrated parents object to paying twice for apparently equivalent required courses at different campuses. From a public policy perspective, proponents of efficient state government were concerned about the "waste" of very limited discretionary state resources that occurs when students are compelled to take duplicate courses at different institutions to fulfill the same requirement. The politics and economics of easing student credit transfer (and minimizing nonessential course redundancy) have often driven state action.

Each of the individual states faced idiosyncratic circumstances that caused transfer and articulation issues to rise on the public policy agenda. In Georgia, the decision of the board of regents to move all public institutions from the quarter to the semester system in 1995 drove a broader effort to develop a system of course equivalencies, which was reflected in the institution of a uniform course numbering system across all public campuses. This larger change led to generating a basic statewide model for the general education requirement. Georgia chose to develop that model inductively, by identifying the common themes among already extant campus general education statements. It also required the establishment of a structure to make "official" judgments about whether courses met uniform state requirements and had equivalent content. While the resulting Council on General Education was originally a procedural enforcer of uniformity, it assumed during the course of this project a key role in raising issues about the intentions and coherence of general education among both academic leaders and faculty members.

In Maryland, articulation issues "piggybacked" on critical statewide reform initiatives in K–16 education. It was within the context of these K–16 initiatives (including the introduction of an associate's degree in teacher preparation) that the question of the goals and purposes of general education among institutions found its way onto the public agenda.

In Utah, what became the Regents' Task Force emerged in 1992 as an ad hoc instrument to review one public campus's request to televise some of its general education offerings. The group, consisting largely of faculty, gradually developed a broader agenda, including the sponsorship of public conversations about the meaning of general education. It was through these self-initiated activities that the task force ultimately positioned itself as a key player when the Utah legislature turned its attention to accountability and assessment as well as, more recently, when a new governor proposed an initiative to enable Utah high school students taking advanced placement courses to enter public postsecondary education as sophomores.

Quite beyond the issue of getting general education onto the public policy agenda of the individual states was the matter of developing in each state a national project agenda and linking that agenda to the agenda in the states. This challenge depended on the leadership of the state-level project coordinators, who were being asked, in effect, not only to solve specific state dilemmas, but also to view their individual state initiatives in the broader context of national trends and issues. For some, the two leadership tasks were taken on coequally; for others, the state context would predominate.

The interests and orientations of leadership primarily affected the propensity of individual states to concurrently take responsibility for a broader national agenda. But such circumstances as support at home and the prior development of state initiatives seem to have been key determinants. In Maryland and Georgia, there was strong central support (including resources) from a powerful state agency. In Utah, maintaining local support and resources for state initiatives (in the absence of any powerful sponsor) monopolized the attention of state coordinators at the expense of national project concerns. Finally, while the Utah project took its shape well before linking to the Greater Expectations for Student Transfer project, the Georgia and Maryland projects were more "opportunistic" and amenable to concurrent definition through the project.

Bringing State Policy to Ground Level

Involving the faculty—that is, ensuring that those who are implementing public policy on the ground understand and act upon statewide intentions—emerged as a formidable challenge. The initiative highlighted the yawning chasm between the senior faculty and department chairs, who disproportionately participate in initiatives at the statewide level, and those teaching general education courses, who are disproportionately part-time and non-tenure-track faculty. Those implementing state general education policy in the classroom are not those typically engaged in the development of such policy. Moreover, those faculty members who are involved at the statewide level tend to be involved as individuals, usually representing their academic fields rather than their campuses. Thus, no structure links statewide representatives to others on their campuses in ways that would ensure awareness of and clarity about general education purposes at the campus level, let alone the departmental level.

Except in Maryland (where the chief academic officers organization has played a key coordinating role), the structures that have emerged for faculty involvement in each state do not systematically connect individual faculty participants with their campuses and academic units. It is important to note, however, that in some fields (English composition, most clearly), there is the cultural expectation that faculty who teach sections of the freshman course regularly work together on syllabus construction and ongoing assessment in a structured, course-specific context. Statewide priorities thereby influence these courses, attenuating what might otherwise be the isolation of part-time and graduate student instructors.

A second strategy for linking state-level to campus structures is to formally connect state projects to campus transfer and advisement officers. Both Georgia and Maryland have reached out to such officers. While this development is promising from the campus perspective, it does nothing to link state initiatives to academic departments and their faculty members.

The Politics of Information

Early on in the project, it became clear that the lack of relevant and timely information at the state level about student course-taking patterns, timely graduation of transfer students, and staffing of general education courses constituted a genuine barrier to any assessment of efforts to increase intentionality and coherence. We did not know which faculty members were teaching general education courses, let alone how they perceived the purposes of general education and how those purposes shaped their syllabi and teaching. We did not know what students thought about their general education experience: whether they were clear about its purposes, where they got that information, and the extent to which they achieved the stated outcomes. We did not know where and when students were taking their general education courses. Nor did we even have a reliable basis for estimating the extent to which transferability of general education courses was getting better and ipso facto leading students to earn their undergraduate degrees more quickly.

Of the three state systems, Georgia's is the most centralized and has the most highly developed information infrastructure. All three states, however, are in various stages of developing a Web-based student advisement system that allows students to identify degree requirements and examine their transcripts in light of these requirements: CAPP in Georgia, ARTSYS in Maryland, and UtahMentor in Utah. An examination of trends in student "hits" of these Web resources suggests that they have become a significantly expanding source of information for students and their parents. To what extent these online resources can serve as a vehicle for conveying general education intentions remains to be seen. Their potential to command the attention of large numbers of students and parents, however, makes them excellent prospective tools for conveying educational intentions. Each course might be prefaced, for example, by a statement of intention and a definition of its role in the educational process.

Logistically, the great strength of these online resources is their relative inexpensiveness and nonintrusiveness. In effect, they rely on students to generate information themselves and adjust their own course selection accordingly, and they are easy to integrate with basic academic transcript and catalog software systems.

In Utah, more generalized information on student perceptions of general education has been provided through the state's experiments with integrating assessment into the student course evaluation process. Most institutions, however, have been reluctant, if for no reason other than institutional inertia, to build on this particular evaluation system, and attempts to pilot similar efforts in both Maryland and Georgia have died on the vine.

Hence, while we began by assuming that an information infrastructure was absolutely essential to building state capability to monitor institutional performance and the effectiveness of public policy, we found that enormous system costs, the high degree of decentralization and institutional autonomy, fears regarding the political volatility of data, and the short attention span of public officials all work against sustaining such effort. In short, information was perceived less often in purely descriptive terms than in political terms. Any realistic effort to build an information infrastructure would require the active management of the political uses of information. That proved to be beyond both our purview and ken.

Sustaining General Education Initiatives at the State Level

If there is one common lesson to be learned in all three states, it is that general education reform has largely operated on a shoestring as an ad hoc initiative. It is sometimes supported with temporary funding for a single fiscal year or for several years via external grants, and it depends, for the most part, on the good will of state-level and campus leadership. Good will can be relied upon to launch new initiatives; however, considerable organizational creativity is needed to translate that good will into effective mechanisms for sustaining attention to ongoing initiatives.

In all three states, structures emerged to sustain attention to issues of intentionality and coherence. In Utah, what had been an ad hoc Regents' Task Force on General Education achieved what can only be described as permanent ad hoc status. The task force gained this status only insofar as its communication activities across stakeholder groups conferred on it a perceived role as a key player in these kinds of policy debates. The group managed to retain its independence from campus administrative and governance structures by maintaining the self-perpetuating character of membership. The task force, rather than campus administrators or state officials, controlled its membership. That meant that the leadership succession function resided in the group itself, and the group was not as easily subject to co-optation by the changing political landscape.

In Georgia, the Council on General Education, which had originally been established by the regents as an enforcer of uniformity in state policy across all public campuses, emerged as a quasi-independent body whose portfolio was expanded to include proactive, self-initiated activities related to clarifying the purposes of general education. This development, however, is attributable most immediately to the leadership of the current state coordinator; it is not clear to what extent, or how, that broader role will be sustained over time in the face of leadership changes.

In Maryland, the quasi-independent character of policy-making structures has not been as clearly developed. While the state's public chief academic officers' organization has taken an umbrella role, the real nucleus of leadership has resided in a few creative administrators at the system office.

These continuing leadership structures, which are perceived as legitimate but not beholden to shifting political sands, become critical because of the political environment of K–16 education in all three states. In Utah, for example, once the pilot assessment programs of general education in three areas was completed, the task force went to the regents and the legislature with a substantial request for resources to institutionalize assessment in the three pilot areas as well as expand to other areas of general education. The legislature's response was twofold. First, legislators took the success of the pilot assessments as an indicator that the institutions were indeed "doing good work" with state tax dollars, which in their view obviated the need to repeat the process. Second, they reinforced the notion that substantial additional public resources would not be forthcoming, and insisted that campuses should reallocate their existing resources to address pressing new needs rather than rely on the state to support resource add-ons as those needs arose.

This response illustrates what emerged as two important determinants of state policy behavior. First, state officials have a short attention span. Once a critical concern has been addressed, it is time to "move on." Second, state officials believe that campuses do not need more money to add new functions. In their view, campuses need rather to restructure what they have been doing to address new public policy concerns.

Some Concluding Thoughts

The story of the national project evaluation is, in some sense, like the public policy process itself: the desired outcomes and indicators of success are articulated, a policy is formulated and implemented, and outcomes are modified as they confront the changing reality of local environments, resulting in the best achievable results. In the case of Greater Expectations for Student Transfer, the project director, in cooperation with the state coordinators, managed to gain commitment to a set of shared national project goals early on and sustain for several years a commitment to self-reflection on project implementation: no small feat. In the process, three states maintained a focus on a set of issues (intentionality and coherence of general education requirements at public systems of higher education) that would not under ordinary circumstances find their way to the top of the public policy agenda. The project succeeded in the basic task of focusing and sustaining the attention of participants on a common agenda.

At the same time, the national project evaluation, no less than the individual state projects, found itself subject to all the political and inter-institutional competitive pressures that typically deflect our singleness of purpose. As a result, the project failed to follow up on data gathering and never fully addressed either the advising system or the students.

Utah and, to a lesser extent, Georgia managed to develop quasi-independent statewide structures to sustain their reform efforts. It is these sorts of structures (and their leaders), relatively insulated from the daily ebbs and flows of the political process and turf defense, that will likely shape the future of general education reform in those states. In some sense, of course, the project evaluation had sought to establish such quasi-independent structures—evaluation teams in each state pairing state or system offices with doctoral students in higher education administration—in the hope that these alliances might be maintained, even informally, as more permanent information infrastructure supports.

Quite beyond focusing and maintaining attention, the project produced some potentially very concrete tools for sustaining general education reform. Each of the three states has developed (more or less under the aegis of the national project) an electronic advising system that allows students to assess their academic programs in terms of progress toward state general education requirements. Each of the three states has also developed the role of campus general education liaisons and structures for bringing those individuals together periodically to monitor the progress of general education reform.

This project encountered very real political and organizational barriers to educational reform and found structures and strategies to surmount those barriers. In that respect, it has made its primary contribution to enhancing the intentionality and coherence of general education.

About the Authors

Chapter 1

Robert Shoenberg, director of the Greater Expectations for Student Transfer project, is a senior fellow at AAC&U. He works as a consultant on matters related to undergraduate education and has written extensively about general and liberal education. His career as a teacher and administrator includes fourteen years as dean for undergraduate studies at the University of Maryland, College Park.

Chapter 2

Ann Leffler was chair of the Utah Regents' Task Force on General Education from 1994 to July 2003. Then a sociologist at Utah State University, she also twice served as dean of the College of Humanities, Arts, and Social Sciences. She is now dean of the College of Liberal Arts and Sciences at the University of Maine. **Philip I. Kramer** was the doctoral student member of the Utah Regents' Task Force on General Education from 2000 to 2003. He is now an assistant professor at the University of Texas at El Paso, where he has a joint appointment in the Departments of Educational Leadership and Foundations and Teacher Education. **Norman L. Jones** is the chair of the history department at Utah State University, the chair of the general education committee at Utah State University, and the current chair of the Utah Regents' Task Force on General Education. **Phyllis "Teddi" Safman**, the assistant commissioner for academic affairs with the Utah State Board of Regents, has among her responsibilities the coherence and assessment of general education, transfer and articulation of academic majors, the Regents' Task Force on Student Success, the federal No Child Left Behind program, and teacher education. Her background includes leadership positions in adult and continuing education nationally, regionally, and statewide, as well as university teaching and music.

Chapter 3

Dorothy D. Zinsmeister is assistant vice chancellor for academic affairs, associate director for higher education–PRISM initiative, and system liaison to the Council on General Education at the Board of Regents of the University System of Georgia.

Chapter 4

Nancy S. Shapiro, associate vice chancellor for academic affairs and director for K–16 partnerships at the University System of Maryland (USM), was the first director of the Maryland K–16 Partnership for Teaching and Learning at USM. As cochair of the K–16 Work Group, she was instrumental in developing the K–16 agenda and charge for the subcommittees and discipline groups. She also designed and developed the secondary associate of arts in teaching implementation agenda. **Teri Hollander,** assistant vice chancellor for academic affairs and director of articulation at USM, established the first chief academic officers group and set the agenda for the development of the general education guidelines for Maryland. She instituted the ARTSYS, a Web-based system at USM that enables all students to access information on the transferability of all courses between the public two-year and four-year colleges in the state. **Jennifer Vest Frank**, director of research at Loyola College, designed and analyzed the AAC&U general education survey while working at the University of Maryland as a graduate assistant.

Chapter 5

Martin Finkelstein, the evaluator for the student transfer project, is professor of higher education at Seton Hall University in South Orange, New Jersey. He has served as a visiting professor at Teachers College, Columbia University, and as a Visiting Scholar at the Claremont Graduate University and Hiroshima University in Japan. He received his doctorate from SUNY at Buffalo. His recent books include *The New Academic Generation* (with Jack Schuster, Johns Hopkins University Press, 1998), *Dollars, Distance and On-Line Education: The New Economics of College Teaching and Learning* (coeditor, ACE Series in Higher Education, 2000), and *The American Faculty* (with Jack Schuster, Johns Hopkins University Press, forthcoming).

About AAC&U

AAC&U is the leading national association concerned with the quality, vitality, and public standing of undergraduate liberal education. Its members are committed to extending the advantages of a liberal education to all students, regardless of academic specialization or intended career. Founded in 1915, AAC&U now comprises 1,000 accredited public and private colleges and universities of every type and size.

AAC&U functions as a catalyst and facilitator, forging links among presidents, administrators, and faculty members who are engaged in institutional and curricular planning. Its mission is to reinforce the collective commitment to liberal education at both the national and local levels and to help individual institutions keep the quality of student learning at the core of their work as they evolve to meet new economic and social challenges.

Information about AAC&U membership, programs, and publications can be found at www.aacu.org.